"In *Crossroads*, Jodie Niznik guides us through the lives of Esther and Jonah and shows us that we, like they, have been called by God for good work that he has prepared for us to do. Niznik encourages us to respond to God by taking a courageous next step to follow him wherever he leads. Each week is filled with outstanding biblical teaching as well as opportunities to consider how these truths apply to our lives. I especially appreciate that Niznik incorporates spiritual practices that enable us to delve deeper into our relationship with the Lord and grow to know, love, and trust him more. This study is a needed invitation to be daringly obedient to God's call on each of our lives."

Sissy Mathew, spiritual formation and teaching pastor at Irving Bible Church

"Jodie's Bible studies are some of my favorite resources! Her insightful and practical application of Scripture keeps her studies at the top of my list. Anyone who uses this Bible study will feel closer to God and better understand his truth."

Kat Armstrong, preacher, author of *The In-Between Place*, and cofounder of The Polished Network

"From time to time, we all stand at crossroads, big ones that alter our life's direction and small ones that keep us on God's good path or divert us onto painful detours. Esther and Jonah stood there too, and each responded differently, teaching us valuable lessons for today. Niznik's fresh approach tells it like it really was . . . and is. For example, she nixes the common Cinderella fairy-tale version of Esther's life. Instead, she reveals the real story behind this sex-trafficked orphan who braved her vile situation to save her people. Each weekly lesson includes a practice session to help us apply gleaned wisdom for navigating our own cross-roads. Jodie's studies move us toward transformative biblical literacy and an action-packed faith that lives what's learned. I trust her studies and you can too."

Sue Edwards, professor at Dallas Theological Seminary and author of the Discover Together Bible Study series

"Every follower of Jesus comes to defining moments of deciding either to follow the whispers of God or to ignore that voice and go our own way. With tremendous skill and insight, Jodie Niznik digs into two remarkable Old Testament stories—Esther and Jonah. This study will stretch and challenge you as Jodie guides with wisdom and practical application each step of the way. I deeply value how Jodie refuses to simply fill our minds with information about the Bible—she consistently pursues the 'So what?' question so we are stirred to action."

NANCY BEACH, leadership coach with the Slingshot Group
and author of *Gifted to Lead*

CROSSROADS

REAL PEOPLE, REAL FAITH BIBLE STUDIES

Choose: A Study of Moses for a Life That Matters

Crossroads: A Study of Esther and Jonah for
Boldly Responding to Your Call

Trust: A Study of Joseph for Persevering
Through Life's Challenges

A
**REAL PEOPLE
REAL FAITH
BIBLE STUDY**

CROSSROADS

*A Study of Esther and Jonah
for Boldly Responding to Your Call*

JODIE NIZNIK

KREGEL
PUBLICATIONS

Crossroads: A Study of Esther and Jonah for Boldly Responding to Your Call
© 2021 by Jodie Niznik

Published by Kregel Publications, a division of Kregel Inc., 2450 Oak Industrial Dr. NE, Grand Rapids, MI 49505.

Library of Congress Cataloging-in-Publication Data
Names: Niznik, Jodie, 1973- author.
Title: Crossroads : a study of Esther and Jonah for boldly responding to
    your call / Jodie Niznik.
Description: Grand Rapids, MI : Kregel Publications, 2021. | Series: Real
    people, real faith Bible studies | Includes bibliographical references.
Identifiers: LCCN 2020045986 (print) | LCCN 2020045987 (ebook) | ISBN
    9780825446733 (print) | ISBN 9780825477232 (epub)
Subjects: LCSH: Vocation--Biblical teaching--Textbooks. | Bible.
    Esther--Textbooks. | Bible. Jonah--Textbooks.
Classification: LCC BS680.V6 N59 2021 (print) | LCC BS680.V6 (ebook) |
    DDC 248.4--dc23
LC record available at https://lccn.loc.gov/2020045986
LC ebook record available at https://lccn.loc.gov/2020045987

ISBN 978-0-8254-4673-3, print
ISBN 978-0-8254-7723-2, epub

Printed in the United States of America
21 22 23 24 25 26 27 28 29 30 / 5 4 3 2 1

To Tim:
thank you for loving me well and
helping me to lean into all the
"for such a time as this" moments,
even when I'd rather head toward Tarshish

CONTENTS

•• • • ••

WHY ESTHER AND JONAH AND WHY NOW?

●●●●●●●

At first glance the books of Esther and Jonah don't seem to go together. They are two separate books about two different people written about three hundred years apart. Esther is the story of an unlikely orphaned girl who becomes queen and through her bravery saves the Jews, her beloved people. Jonah is the story of a reluctant prophet who ran from God but then eventually conceded to God's will. He was also called to save an entire group of people, his enemies, the Ninevites. Esther's bravery is easy to admire. Jonah's running is easy to condemn.

While Esther and Jonah endured wildly different circumstances and had distinctly different callings, they were both providentially born in a certain time and place in history. They were carried through unique experiences and given specific gifts. And then God placed each of them at a crossroads and asked them to fulfill an assignment that only they could, but God also gave them the choice to bravely obey . . . or not.

This wasn't just true for Esther and Jonah; it's also true for you. You, too, have been called by God to do good work that he has already prepared for you (Ephesians 2:10). He has given you gifts and skills. He has brought you through experiences, both good and bad, and he has placed you in this time and space in history. All of these factors point to the fact that there is work not only that you have been called to do but that only you can do. And now you stand at a crossroads. What will you choose?

I want us to study Esther and Jonah together because not only have we been called and chosen by God, but we also have a little bit of Esther and Jonah in each of us. There are days when we make bold, brave, and admirable decisions to follow God's leading like Esther did. And then there are days when we run the other way like Jonah did. Even though they lived centuries ago, their lives have much to teach us about following God's calling on our lives today.

My prayer is that through this study of Esther and Jonah you would know the deep truth that you are chosen and called. I'm also praying that God would reveal a next step for you to take along his chosen path for you, and that you would have the courage to take it. Just like Esther and Jonah, you have been called to do good work. As you stand at your crossroads, may you follow him boldly and bravely on the journey.

—Jodie

WHAT TO EXPECT IN THIS STUDY

• • • • • • •

Practice Sections

Each week our lesson will start with a short practice section. The word *practice* is simple and to me expresses the idea that we are just trying something out in our relationship with the Lord. We are practicing. This section will also be a place for us to reflect on the truths we are learning and bring them into our lives in a new way. These practices won't take huge amounts of time, but they may require some planning. Therefore, we will start each week's lesson with the practice section, read it through, and then make a plan to try the suggested activities.

You may discover something you really love in these little sections—something that brings new life into your relationship with the Lord. You may also discover that some of these exercises will take effort. Some may be hard for you to do and others may be easy, even fun! But all of them will help you stretch and grow. Growth almost always brings the spiritual fruit of a changed life. For me, that makes any effort totally worth it. I hope you agree. I'm actually guessing you do. Otherwise, you wouldn't be starting this study.

Pacing Your Study

Each week of this study includes a practice for the week, an introduction to prepare you for the material, and three study sessions. You are welcome to tackle as much of the week's material as you would like on any given day. However, I suggest giving yourself five days to complete the week's work, and I have marked the sections accordingly. If you break it into these chunks, the study shouldn't take you more than thirty minutes to do each day. However, if you are a researcher or extensive reflective thinker, you may want to set aside more time for each day's study.

In general, you will find the days broken down as follows:

Day one will be reading about and planning for the practice activity.

Days two through five will be Scripture reading and answering the questions in this study guide.

If you start running behind (we all have those weeks), you may have to pick and choose which questions you want to answer. My advice is to make the Scripture reading your first priority. Then if you have time, scan through the questions to see which ones you want to answer.

As is usually the case, the higher the investment, the greater the return. When we collaborate with Jesus by inviting him into our lives and spending time with him, we experience life transformation. As your life is transformed, you will find it looking more and more like the life God designed you to live. So make every effort to arrange your days so that you can regularly spend time with Jesus.

ESTHER BECOMES QUEEN

Day 1
Practice—Noticing Our Unseen God

Each week before we start our lesson, I will offer an activity to help you take another step in your relationship with the Lord. These brief exercises take head knowledge you are learning from God's Word and move it into heart knowledge.

I know it can be really tempting to skip these if you feel pressed for time, but can I encourage you not to? Sometimes these short activities are exactly what our soul needs. Often they take very little time and just a bit of intentionality.

This week we will engage in a practice to help us notice our unseen God. As you'll discover, God is the unseen main character of the book of Esther, and he is also the unseen main character of our lives. Because he is unseen, we can easily miss him even though he's still there and still working. He's often working through the ordinariness of our lives. Most of the time it isn't through miracles, as we might recognize them, but through the seemingly mundane things.

For example, just a few minutes ago I needed a quick sunshine

break, so I headed out to the backyard. There I found a beautiful
and perfect tomato ready for me to pick off one of our vines. Yes,
I know, it's just a tomato, and it was supposed to grow because
my husband planted it and tended it. But in that moment as I
crouched by the vine, I paused and noticed. It led to a brief holy
moment that pointed me to the creator of all creation. I noticed
my unseen God, and I marveled at him and his provision for me.

Now it's your turn to do some noticing. Take a few minutes
before you start each day's lesson to write down three to five
instances where you noticed God over the last twenty-four hours.
I recommend that you think through your day chronologically,
starting with waking up in the morning. Ask the Lord to help
you notice him. It might be through a coincidence, a circumstance, something in nature, someone's kindness, an answered
prayer, or something else. Write down what you notice and then
praise him for how he was present in your day.

Here's a little prayer you can pray to help you get started:
"Lord, help me notice you. Spirit, guide me to see where you are
and how you have been working in my life. Thank you that you
love me enough to be in my moments and days even when I don't
notice you. Help me to notice you now. Amen."

What are three to five ways you've noticed God was present in
the last twenty-four hours?

1.

2.

3.

4.

5.

PRACTICE REMINDER

Pray and ask the Lord to help you notice
three to five places where he was present over
the last twenty-four hours. Write them below.

1.

2.

3.

4.

5.

Day 2
How Did We Get Here?

The Book of Esther
Author: *Unknown*
Date Written: *Unknown, but sometime after 460 BC and
likely before 200 BC*
Purpose: *Esther was written to remind the Jewish people who
remained in exile that God had not forgotten them.*

Before we start our study of Esther, we need to understand a
little bit about the background and history of the book. I know
some of you just perked up when I said history and the rest of you

scanned down to see exactly how long this history lesson would be. I'm part of the scanning crowd, if it makes you feel any better, so I'll keep this brief. Before we can start to understand any book of Scripture, it's important to know a little bit about the audience it was written to, when it was written, and why.

So, let's start with some historical background. About a thousand years before Esther's story began, God made a covenant (called the Mosaic covenant) with his people, the Israelites, through Moses. This binding and holy promise essentially said that if the nation of Israel followed the laws and commands of God, he would provide for them and protect them. If, however, they didn't follow his laws and commands, then he would allow their enemies to attack and scatter them (Deuteronomy 28:15, 64).

If you know anything about biblical history concerning the nation of Israel, you know that the Israelites were an on-again, off-again people. When they were off, which was frequently, they wandered away from God, even going so far as to worship other gods. And yet God was patient. Exceedingly so. He would lovingly pursue them until they would eventually repent and return to him. This wandering away from and returning to God repentance cycle repeated again and again . . . for about eight hundred years.

Until one day, near 586 BC, the Lord allowed the consequences of their disobedience to unfold. This quickly became one of the darkest hours and lowest moments for the nation of Israel. The powerful, fierce, and unrelenting Babylonians overtook the city of Jerusalem and exiled the Jewish people, scattering them throughout the land, just as Moses had said would happen. Esther's family was moved to the city of Susa (modern-day Iran). During this time, the Babylonians also destroyed the holy temple. To the Israelites this destruction was devastating because it represented God's very presence with his people. The Israelites saw, in a physical way, that God had removed his hand of protection from them and had left them on their own. This leaving, of course, was symbolic. God never fully left his people. He was always willing and wanting to take them back. But near

586 BC the nation was left scattered and wondering what would be next.

About fifty years later, a new king came to rule over Babylon. He favored the Israelites and allowed them to return to their homeland, Jerusalem, and begin to rebuild. Many Jews returned home, but others, like Esther's family, had established new lives and, understandably, decided to stay in their new cities.

Near 485 BC (another fifty years in the future), we find ourselves in the story told in the book of Esther, which is set in the city of Susa. Susa was the hub of the Persian Empire, and the home of the powerful King Xerxes. Xerxes wasn't just any king—he was probably the most powerful man, and one of the wealthiest, alive at the time. This meant everything, including people, was at his disposal. King Xerxes was also an overindulgent, impulsive, prideful people-pleaser. Sounds like a great leader, doesn't he? And this is where Esther, our unlikely hero, lived.

Understanding this history is important because it points to one of the major themes of the book of Esther: Has God forgotten his people? Other books of Scripture written around this same time—1 and 2 Chronicles, Haggai, Zechariah, Ezra, and Nehemiah—address this question toward the Jews who had returned to rebuild their lives in Jerusalem. These books reminded them that their God is a covenant-keeping and faithful God, in spite of their inability to keep the covenant or be faithful. The book of Esther addresses this question toward the Jews who were still in exile, reminding them that they too were still held by God in his covenant and faithfulness. They had also not been forgotten.

Depending on your Bible translation, King Xerxes may be referred to as King Ahasuerus. This is because his Persian name was actually Khshayarshan, which when translated into Hebrew becomes Ahasuerus and when translated into Greek becomes Xerxes. Since we're primarily using the NIV translation in this study, we'll use King Xerxes, the NIV's name for him.

A quick read through Esther reveals something very interesting:

there is no mention of God in the entire text. In fact, Esther is the only book of Scripture that doesn't explicitly mention God. The absence is glaring. Where is he? As you will see, he is actually everywhere. He is the unseen main character who orchestrates every moment, every twist, and every "coincidence."

"When we speak of God's providence, we mean that God, in some invisible and inscrutable way, governs all creatures, actions, and circumstances through the normal and ordinary course of human life, without the intervention of the miraculous."
—Karen H. Jobes[1]

This points to another one of the main themes of the book: the providential care of God. *Providence* simply means that God is working in our normal lives, providing care and provision even when we can't see him. He is in control; he always is. Many believe the purposeful lack of mentioning God is part of the genius behind Esther, because even when he isn't named, he is still there. He is unseen but holding everything together. This is true for our lives as well.

As we tackle the book of Esther, it's important to remember that it is a story. Like any story it has a narrative arc—a beginning that sets the stage and introduces the characters, a middle that is full of tension and drama, and an end that brings resolution. Because the book of Esther is short, I want us to read the whole story before we start to dissect it. It should take you less than thirty minutes to read all 167 verses, and then just think, you can brag to your friends that you read a whole book in one sitting today.

If you don't have time to read the whole book in one sitting, try googling "Esther audio Bible" and let someone read it to you.

Read or listen to the entire book of Esther. Write down anything that stands out to you or that you have questions about.

PRACTICE REMINDER

Pray and ask the Lord to help you notice three
to five places where he was present over the last
twenty-four hours. Write them below.

1.

2.

3.

4.

5.

Day 3
Setting the Stage
Read Esther 1:1–12.

1. What do you learn about King Xerxes in these verses? (Consider the banquets, the opulence, summoning the queen, and his response when she didn't come.)

✺

"Xerxes lived for his own pleasure; a walking, talking, wielding, threatening example of the lust of the flesh, lust of the eyes, and the pride of life. The author of Esther is careful to describe in detail the sumptuousness of Xerxes's palace, the excess of drinking, and the insane amount of splendor that took half a year to view (1:4)."

—Sharifa Stevens[2]

2. Consider Queen Vashti. What do you think it would be like to be summoned by seven of the king's servants to go to the king's banquet? Why do you think she said no? Do you think she understood the potential consequences?

3. Regardless of why she decided not to go when summoned, Queen Vashti showed great courage in saying no to the king. Where have you seen someone show great courage recently? How does this embolden you?

4. The consequences for Queen Vashti refusing to go before King Xerxes were risky (verse 19). Have you ever refused to do something that resulted in costly consequences? Describe what happened. Would you make the same decision again? Why or why not?

Queen Vashti was summoned by seven servants of the king to be presented to hundreds of entitled and powerful men who had been getting drunk for days. The queen was vastly outnumbered on all fronts. I wonder if, in the moment, disobeying the king seemed like a far safer option than entering that room.

....

Read Esther 1:13–22.

5. The king's advisors recommended King Xerxes take decisive and bold action. What were they afraid might happen (verses 17–18)? Why do you think they feared this?

As a result, the king issued an edict that deposed Vashti of her queenship and banished her from ever seeing the king again. This edict also impacted every woman in the kingdom as it proclaimed that every man ruled over his household (verse 22). This edict was supposed to command women to respect their husbands (verse 20).

6. Read Jesus's words in Matthew 7:12 and 22:39. Based on this and other things you know of Jesus's teachings, how do you think Jesus would advocate for us to earn another person's respect? How does this contrast with how Xerxes was trying to gain respect?

7. Think of someone you greatly respect. Why do you respect them? Does this align more with Jesus's words or the king's advisors?

PRACTICE REMINDER

Pray and ask the Lord to help you notice three
to five places where he was present over the last
twenty-four hours. Write them below.

1.

2.

3.

4.

5.

Day 4
Mordecai and Hadassah

Read Esther 2:1–7.

Later the king's anger subsided, and he realized what he had done
and that he needed a new queen. This is where we meet Esther.
There are a few things to note about her before we get too far
into her story.

First, Esther was an orphaned Jewish girl with no power, no
standing, and no rights. She was essentially a nobody, at least to
the king and anyone else with power or standing. And yet, as we

will see, Esther was also a woman called by God to save an entire nation. She prevented a genocide. She protected the lineage of King Jesus. She wasn't a nobody to God, and she teaches us that when our God moves, nothing can stop him.

Second, Esther was a trafficked woman. She was a woman taken against her will to be used at the whim of someone more powerful than she was. This should make us sad, angry, even sick. It should also provoke us to rise up to remember and fight for those impacted by similar atrocities today. Anyone who tries to pass this off as a love story or beauty pageant is missing the point.

Finally, Esther was an image bearer of God. While the unspeakable was happening to her, God didn't turn away. He was with her, and honestly that's hard to reconcile. But he was there. She was still his beloved, and he helped her rise up in the midst of it all to follow him for a greater purpose. Esther is, in many ways, my hero. I don't want her story—none of us do—but I want to be more like her. She was brave and bold. She kept her eyes set on God. She didn't let the personification of evil destroy her. I can't wait to meet her in heaven and give her a big hug, to cry righteous tears with her, and to celebrate victory with her.

This is our Esther. Let's dive in and learn from her.

8. Describe how the new queen would be selected. As a woman, how do you feel about the king's plan?

9. According to verses 5 through 7, what do you learn about Mordecai? Why do you think the author of Esther makes sure we know these details about Mordecai?

10. According to these verses, what do you learn about Hadassah (Esther)? Why do you think this is important?

"In Hebrew narrative the physical attributes described when a character is first introduced is of special relevance to his or her role in the story. By describing Esther's beauty, the author is aligning her with the women already mentioned in the story, beautiful queen Vashti and the beautiful young virgins, thus creating a certain expectation for how Esther will fare in the Persian court." —Karen H. Jobes[3]

Read Esther 2:8–14.

11. Do you think Esther had a choice in going to the king's palace? Why or why not? Regardless of whether she had a choice, how did she seem to act once she got there (verse 9)?

Mordecai forbids Esther from revealing her nationality or family background. The text doesn't indicate if King Xerxes would have cared that she was Jewish. In fact, it only seems to point out that he held shallow standards of beauty, pleasure, and submission as his criteria for the new

"The verb [*taken*] does not suggest 'anything unpleasant', but it is impossible to know whether she went without reluctance. It is questionable whether any woman could exercise the right of choice in the face of a royal order."
—Joyce G. Baldwin[4]

queen. However, even if it didn't matter to him, it mattered to those around him and apparently Mordecai knew this.

The other thing that is interesting to note about Esther keeping her identity a secret is that it also means she no longer followed the Jewish dietary laws. The text tells us that Hegai, who had charge of the harem, provided her with special food. We have to assume that it was not in compliance with Jewish regulations. Why would it be? After all, he had no idea she was Jewish. Daniel, another famous Bible character, when faced with a similar situation, refuses to eat food that isn't in compliance with the dietary regulations. The Lord blesses both Esther and Daniel in these very different circumstances. I love that there isn't always one right answer. To me this emphasizes the importance of our relationship with God. We need to continually seek him and what's best in each situation. God asked Daniel to refrain from eating the rich foods offered him, and through the counsel of Mordecai, God asked Esther to blend in. Both were following God's best in their specific situations.

12. How do you think Esther was able to keep her identity a secret? Are there people in our society who hide their nationality and family background today? Why do you think they do this?

13. Think back over your life. When have you hidden or been tempted to hide something about your identity (race, age, birthplace, family of origin, personality traits, vocation, etc.)? Describe the situation and why you felt you needed to hide.

14. Xerxes, as a king, had a distorted view of Esther's dignity and worth, but this is not how God, our heavenly King, viewed her or how he views any of us. Compare Xerxes's view of Esther with God's view of Esther by filling in the chart below.

King Xerxes's View	God's View
Esther is a commodity with the sole purpose to serve my desires and whims.	Ephesians 2:10 Esther is:
Esther's body is only for my pleasure.	1 Corinthians 6:19 Esther's body is:
Esther should give herself for me.	Romans 5:8 Esther, I will:
Esther needs to fight for a place in the palace.	Philippians 3:20 Esther is:

15. Go back to the chart you just filled in and read God's truths again, but this time put your name where Esther's is. Do this slowly and prayerfully, asking the Lord if you have a distorted view of yourself that he needs to correct with his loving truth. Is there one truth that stands out to you? How does this truth combat a distorted view you may be holding?

PRACTICE REMINDER

Pray and ask the Lord to help you notice three
to five places where he was present over the last
twenty-four hours. Write them below.

1.

2.

3.

4.

5.

Day 5
One Night with the King

Read Esther 2:15–18.

At this point in the story, four years have passed since Xerxes
banished Vashti. Esther won the favor of Hegai, the king's eunuch
in charge of the harem, and made the choice to follow both his
and Mordecai's advice to prepare for her time with the king. The
beauty treatments were meant to be preparation for marriage,
but as Joyce Baldwin noted in her commentary, "For the majority
what awaited them was more like widowhood than marriage."[5]

Only one woman would become queen. The rest of the women would become concubines, mistresses to the king, where most would likely be forgotten.

16. According to these verses, what happened to Esther and why? What were the reasons Xerxes chose her over the other women? How do you see this same thing happening today in our world? How can this distort women's value and worth?

17. Esther was made queen instead of Vashti. How did King Xerxes celebrate? What do you think it was like for the people in the kingdom?

18. Knowing we can't really put ourselves in Esther's shoes since she lived in a day and culture so different from ours, and since the text doesn't give us any clues about how she felt about being selected as queen, I'd still like to invite you to take a moment to consider everything that has happened to her up to this point. Write down what you think she might have been thinking and feeling about becoming queen, both good and bad.

"The king's generosity even touched the common people. . . .
It's likely that taxes were canceled, servants set free, and work-
ers given a vacation from their jobs. [Xerxes] wanted everybody
to feel good about his new queen." —Warren W. Wiersbe[6]

19. Providence, one of the key themes in the book of Esther,
    is God's active and intimate involvement in sustaining our
    world and providing for the needs of people, especially
    those who follow him in faith, even when we don't clearly
    see his involvement. Looking back over this week's lesson
    and the verses we covered, where do you see the providence
    of God in action?

20. How does understanding God's providence impact how
    you will follow him the next time you find yourself at a
    crossroads and feel led to follow God in a new direction?

PRACTICE REFLECTION

Look back over your notes from this week's daily practice of noticing God presence and provision.

1. How do the things you noted reveal the providence of God in your own life?

2. What stands out to you about how God provided for you this week?

EDICT OF DEATH

Day 1
Practice—Fasting and Prayer

Esther may have been called by God for a significant task, but it's hard to overlook that she was a trafficked woman—there isn't any way around it. She lived in a day and time where women had little choice. When she was summoned by the king to the palace, there was nothing she could do about it. While some women in her day may have welcomed this as an opportunity to live in luxury, we have no way of knowing how Esther felt about it. For those women who did welcome it, it most likely didn't turn out to fulfill their hopes or dreams. They had one night with the king, and then they were discarded into his harem for a lifetime. Forever at the king's beck and call, but most would never have an audience with the king again.

Here's the problem: This didn't just happen in Esther's day. Around the world and in our own communities, women are being taken, sold, and abused every day. It's hard to get accurate statistics because no one really knows how many women have been silenced and hidden away. However, if you run any kind of an internet search, the available statistics are all alarming. These are our sisters. They deserve better.

There are many good people out there fighting to end human trafficking and restore human dignity. I'm so grateful for these passionate people, but honestly, when I start to think of this issue, the problem feels insurmountable and I become immobilized. I think, "But I'm just one person. What can I really do that would make a difference? Where do I even start?" If I'm honest, I'll tell you that I'm also a little afraid. What will I find when I start looking? What will happen to my heart when the statistics are no longer simply numbers but become flesh-and-blood human beings?

I'm not really sure how to answer all those questions, but I do know this: ignoring the issue won't make the problem go away. I think we've all heard some version of this saying: "The only thing necessary for the triumph of evil is that good men [and women] should do nothing."[1] Truth. Doing nothing means evil gains ground. As believers, we look forward to the day when Jesus will return to set all these evil things right, but while we wait, we are called to combat the evil we see around us today (Psalm 82:3–4). So let's at least do something—even a small something. Whether it's praying, donating resources, or moving to the front lines, there is something each of us can do.

This brings us to our practice for the week. On day 5 this week you will read that Esther invited the community to fast and pray with her before she went to the king uninvited to beg for his mercy. Fasting was a common practice in Esther's day and is seen practiced throughout Scripture. People fasted for many reasons, but mainly it was to draw near to God as they sought his strength, favor, or direction. We fast for similar reasons today. While fasting is no guarantee that we will receive what we are seeking, it is an effective way to focus our hearts toward God as we boldly petition him. Fasting is never wasted. This week, in solidarity with all people who are victims of human trafficking, I want to invite you to fast and pray boldly on their behalf. There are a lot of ways you can do this. Here are some ideas:

- Fast from social media. Every time you think to pick up your phone to browse or post, spend time praying for trafficked and abused people instead.

- Fast from buying something you want or even need—coffee, meals, clothing—and donate that money to a trusted organization that is fighting against trafficking.

- Fast from one or more meals and spend that time praying or serving. If you would have spent money on that meal, consider donating it to a trusted organization.

This is by no means a complete list of ways one can fast. Pray about how God might want you to help vulnerable people, and feel free to be creative. What does the Lord bring to mind? Do that thing. Earnest and genuine prayers are effective because we pray to a God who is providential. He sees each and every person who has been taken. He knows her or his name and the number of hairs on their head. He calls each person beloved even though evil people want to label them a commodity to be used and discarded.

Our prayers and actions actually make a difference, so let's do something. In this case, it's always better than doing nothing.

Take a moment to write down your plan for your practice this week.

If you'd like a suggestion for a trustworthy organization to support, one I trust is My Refuge House. They are located in the Philippines and have the motto "Restoring One Life at a Time." I was able to visit a few years ago to meet some of the precious young, much too young, girls who were living there. Their resilience and joy testify to the miraculous redemption God can do in lives. It's slow work, though. My Refuge House is doing this slow work of restoring, re-mothering, and reeducating young girls who have been trafficked. You can find out more at myrefugehouse .com. Thankfully there are a lot of great organizations out there doing this kind of work—because, unfortunately, there is a lot of work to do.

Remember to practice fasting
and praying this week.

Day 2
A Plot Exposed

Read Esther 2:19–23.

In this passage, Mordecai, Esther's father figure, had been moved into an official role at the palace. It is unclear if Esther used her influence to make this happen. Regardless, Mordecai was sitting at the king's gate in an official role. In ancient times, the gate would have been more like a building that led into the palace than an actual gate as we would picture one. The gate was also where much official business took place. Mordecai sitting at the gate would allow him access to hear what was going on. The two men mentioned in verse 21, Bigthana and Teresh, were guarding the door to the king's residence, which means they had direct access to the king.

1. What does verse 20 say Esther did? What do you think this says about Esther and Mordecai's relationship?

The fact that Esther kept her ethnicity and relationship with Mordecai a secret becomes an important point to remember for our next lesson.

2. What plot did Mordecai uncover and how did he respond? What did Esther then do? What, in turn, happened to Bigthana and Teresh? What do you think this decisive and irrevocable reaction reveals about King Xerxes?

Typically Persian kings rewarded acts of loyalty quickly and abundantly. Mordecai's good deeds were recorded in the annals—the king's historical records—but went unrewarded and unrecognized by the king. I doubt Mordecai warned the king with the sole hope of receiving a reward, but I'm sure he still noticed he didn't get one. And Mordecai, just like us, would have enjoyed whatever the reward would have been.

3. Read Matthew 6:1–4. What does this passage say we should do when we are doing good deeds? How does this passage encourage you when your good deeds aren't recognized?

Read Esther 3:1–6.

Cue the villain.

In this passage we are introduced to Haman, another one of the main characters of our story. Haman was identified as an Agagite, which means he was a descendant of Agag, the king of the Amalekites. This means that he and Mordecai are age-old enemies. Let me explain.

The Amalekites were the first nation to wage war against the Israelites back in the days of Moses, so more than a thousand years prior to Esther's life. During this epic battle, the Israelites were winning whenever Moses held up his hands on the hill overlooking the battle. As the war raged on, Moses's arms grew tired and he lowered them. As soon as this happened, the Amalekites started winning. So, two men, Aaron and Hur, came to Moses's aid and held his arms up, which enabled the Israelites to win the battle. At the end of the battle the Lord declared he would "be at war against the Amalekites from generation to generation" (Exodus 17:16).

About four hundred years later, God was ready to end the ongoing and dangerous feud between the Amalekites and the Israelites, so he commanded King Saul to completely destroy the Amalekites. Saul, however, disobeyed God. He destroyed all the Amalekites, except one. He decided to preserve the king's life. This king was named Agag—and Haman is a direct descendant of his (1 Samuel 15:1–3, 8).

Haman carried a deep-seated and generations-long hatred for the Jews. Mordecai, being a Jew, was immediately in his crosshairs.

"Each year on the Feast of Purim, the Book of Esther is read publicly in the synagogue; and whenever the reader mentions Haman's name, the people stamp their feet and exclaim, 'May his name be blotted out!' To Jews everywhere, Haman personifies everybody who has tried to exterminate the people of Israel."

—Warren W. Wiersbe[2]

4. Not only does Mordecai get overlooked for his good deed that saved the king, but who does King Xerxes honor instead (Esther 3:1)? Have you ever experienced someone receiving credit for your work or on the heels of your work? What happened? How did this make you feel?

I think it's interesting to note that in the literary flow of this story, we learned that Mordecai saved King Xerxes in 2:22–23 and that the king was fully aware of this. The expected reaction would be for Xerxes to honor and elevate this kind of loyalty. And so as we move into chapter three, we should expect verse 1 to say, "After these events, King Xerxes honored Mordecai." And yet, it doesn't. It says he honored Haman. The author is intentionally drawing our attention to Haman and Mordecai by putting these events back to back with this unexpected twist. This is a classic case of good versus evil. And for the moment, it seems like evil is winning. But since you've read the whole story, you already know that evil doesn't win.

This makes me think of where we are in history. Sometimes it feels like evil is winning, but we know the rest of the story. Jesus wins. (If you aren't familiar with this part of the story, check out 1 Corinthians 15:55–57 and Revelation 21:3–7.) In fact, he already won when his resurrection defeated sin and death. The enemy can take his shots, but his power is limited. Jesus will return and set things right. I long for this day. I know we all do. In the meantime, remember that we know how our story really ends.

5. Haman is honored by being promoted to second in power to the king. What did Haman expect the people to do, and how did Mordecai respond (verses 1–4)? The text doesn't tell us, but what are some of the possible reasons Mordecai responded as he did?

6. When Haman found out Mordecai was a Jew, what did he set out to do (verses 5–6)? Considering the history of the Agagites and the Israelites, what do you think of Haman's reaction? How did the king comply (verse 11)?

PRACTICE REMINDER

Remember to practice fasting
and praying this week.

Day 3
Declaring the Day of Death

Read Esther 3:7–15.

Haman cast lots, which look like modern dice and were used to make decisions, to determine when the genocide would happen. The lots determined Haman would have to wait eleven long months before he could fulfill his heinous plans. However, he immediately sent terror through the land as he notified and ordered that all Jews, including women and children, were to be destroyed, and plundered on the thirteenth day of the twelfth month (verse 13). Ironically, this was the day before the Passover, which is the day the Jews commemorate their miraculous deliverance from slavery under the Egyptians.

It's hard to say why the Jews didn't take this eleven-month window as an opportunity to pack up and flee. It may be they didn't have anywhere to go or they didn't want to leave their livelihoods behind. Or perhaps they were not allowed to leave. Or maybe they believed God would deliver them like he did on the first Passover. Whatever the reason, they stayed.

7. According to verse 15, after the couriers were sent out, what did Haman and King Xerxes do next? Why do you think they did this and what do you think it says about them? How did the city of Susa respond?

8. Imagine you were a Jew living under King Xerxes's rule. How do you think you would feel knowing you would be killed in eleven months by your neighbors? What kind of tensions do you think this would create?

9. The Jews obviously didn't know the rest of their story, so it probably felt like evil was winning as they walked through the next days and months under their declared death sentence. What are some places where it seems like evil is winning in your world today? How are you responding to these situations? What truths do you need to remember and declare about these situations?

Read Esther 4:1–9.

10. How did Mordecai respond (verses 1–2)? How did the other Jews throughout the provinces respond (verse 3)? How do you think you would have responded?

11. The city was in turmoil, yet Esther seemed to not know the edict even existed due to her being sheltered and protected within the castle walls. How did Esther find out about the edict (verses 5–9)? What did Mordecai ask Esther to do? How do you think she felt when she found out about the edict? How do you think she felt about Mordecai's request?

12. Hathak, one of the king's eunuchs assigned to Esther, talked to Mordecai and then delivered the news to her. He seemed like a relatively small and insignificant player in this whole drama, but he wasn't. What actions could he have taken instead of doing what Mordecai requested? How might this have impacted the rest of the story?

13. Think of some other relatively "small" and "insignificant" players recorded in Scripture. What are some of the things they did? (Here are a few verses to get you started: Luke 21:1–4; 23:23–26; and John 6:5–11.) How did their actions impact God's story? How does this encourage you in the role you play in God's story?

Remember to practice fasting
and praying this week.

Day 4
For Such a Time as This

Read Esther 4:10–14.

14. What did Esther tell Mordecai could happen to her if she
    went to the king? How long had it been since she had seen
    the king? What could this mean about her relationship with
    Xerxes?

15. Mordecai gave Esther three reasons why she should boldly
    go to the king in verses 13 and 14. What were they? Which
    one seems most compelling to you? Why?

Mordecai stated, "And who knows but that you have come to your
royal position for such a time as this?" Talk about a crossroads
moment. We have the benefit of knowing the rest of the story

and that she was in fact called by God for this exact moment. Esther did not know this, though. She had no way of knowing what would happen. She could have been killed by Xerxes on the spot, her words may not have made a difference, or something else unpredictable could have happened.

16. How do you think Esther was feeling about all the decisions she faced? If you were Esther, what emotions do you think you would be feeling and what thoughts do you think you would be thinking?

Given the time and place we live in, we will probably never have to confront the possibility of dying for our obedience to God as Esther did. However, I believe we will have many "for such a time as this" crossroads moments. Times when we reach our own crossroads and have the opportunity to step out boldly to take a risk in obedience to God's calling.

17. Reflect back over your life. When have you obediently taken a leap of faith? What felt risky about this for you? What happened? Would you call these "for such a time as this" moments? Why or why not?

18. Just like Hathak and Esther, we too are called by God to do
    large and small acts of obedience. Take a moment to pray
    and ask the Lord if there is something he is inviting you to
    do in obedience to him (for example: make a big or small
    change to your life, speak out or speak up about something,
    serve or give in a new way, etc.). What is it? Make a plan
    to do what you believe he is inviting you to do. Consider
    sharing this with your group for accountability and prayer.

If you don't feel like you're getting a sense of leading on what
God may be calling you to do next, go back to the basics of what
you already know is true of him and his calling on your life—to
love him and love others well (Matthew 22:37–39). While there
are times when we get the sense that God is calling us to join
him in a bigger work that could require a total life change, more
often God invites us to just take the next baby step. To do the
next right thing.

This doesn't mean that these next right steps, even small steps,
are easy. Far from it. Often they are sacrificial and inconvenient.
Sometimes when I am praying a name will come to mind that I
haven't thought of for a while. I'll ask the Lord what he wants
me to do about it—and sometimes I get nothing so I just pray
for them. Other times, though, I get the sense he wants me to
reach out to them or do something for them. This is often, if not
always, inconvenient. I rarely have extra time in my day. And
if I'm honest, I'll tell you I get a little unnerved by just reaching
out to someone I haven't talked to for a while to see how they
are and if they need anything. I jump to the worst-case scenario
and think, "What if they need everything?" And yet every time
I follow through, they usually just need encouragement. And for
them to hear, "God put you on my heart today. I think maybe he
just wants you to know he loves you and he sees you." It is always

life-giving for people. I certainly want to hear these words, don't you?

I think it's worth noting that God will accomplish his purposes with or without us. If we let fear or busyness derail or distract us from what we feel he is inviting us to do, then he will still do what needs to be done, but we will miss out on the joy of being a part of his plan. Don't get me wrong, there may be consequences for us and the people around us, but God's bigger purposes and plans will always be fulfilled.

Take it from me, you don't want to miss out on the joy of being a part of what God is doing. I've done it too many times and I always regret not responding to the God promptings in my life. If you feel like he's placed you at a crossroads, then boldly and bravely follow where you think he is leading. Even if it doesn't turn out the way you think it should, you will know that you didn't turn away from God's invitation—and this, while often inconvenient, is always worth it.

Remember to practice fasting
and praying this week.

Day 5
Fasting and Praying

Read Esther 4:15–17.

Esther asked the community to fast with her for three days. Although prayer was not mentioned, it is very much implied. All fasting by Jews would have been connected to prayer. Once this was done, she went to see the king as she boldly declared, "If I perish, I perish."

19. Esther invited the community to be with her in this important endeavor. What are some specific ways community has played an important role in your faith journey? How do you think your faith would be different without this community?

20. Pray and ask the Lord if there is someone you need to be more intentional about praying for and supporting. Take five minutes to write this person a handwritten note and prayer to encourage them.

21. Providence, as a reminder, is God's active and intimate involvement in sustaining our world and providing for the needs of people, especially those who follow him in faith, even when we don't clearly see it. Look back over this lesson and write down some of the places where you see God's providence at work in the story of Esther.

PRACTICE REFLECTION

1. How has God led you to fast and pray this week?

2. What was that experience like for you?

3. Did you learn anything new about yourself or God and his heart for people as a result of this practice? If so, what?

FACING THE CROSSROADS

Day 1

Practice—Loving the Vulnerable

Have you noticed that Esther told almost no one who she really was? She was queen, yet she hid her true identity. No one knew her heritage, her ethnicity, or her lineage. On the advice of her adopted father, Mordecai, she kept all of this a secret. As we quickly see, there was good reason for her to hide her true identity, and sadly history has taught many of us to do the same.

I remember studying the Holocaust when I was younger. I recall feeling so bewildered as I tried to wrap my mind around why this group of people was hated so much that they were systematically and brutally killed. One of my best friends was Jewish, and she and her family were amazing, generous, and kind. Why would someone want to kill people just because of their national and religious heritage? It made no sense to me.

Later when I started studying the Bible, I came to realize it had nothing to do with how awesome my friends were. It had everything to do with the good versus evil battle that started when sin made its way into our world. As soon as God stated that he would save all people through the birth of his Son, the enemy set his sights on the chosen group designated to bear this Savior. Hatred for the Jewish people has simmered and flared ever since.

Of course, the enemy lost the ultimate battle of trying to snuff out the lineage of Jesus. It was a battle he actually didn't even have a chance of winning because what our God says will happen, will happen. He's God. He wins. Always.

But sadly, the enemy hasn't given up on his tactics of causing division and dissension among people, Jewish or otherwise. He figures, if he's going down (which he is), he's going to cause as much chaos as he can along the way. One of the ways the enemy causes chaos is through stirring up ethnic and social tension. These tensions are just as bad today as they were in Esther's day. Just like Esther, it's common for people who feel vulnerable to hide who they really are.

But God is clear that all people are equally chosen, equally beloved, and equally valued. Galatians says it this way, "There is neither Jew nor Gentile, neither slave nor free, nor is there male and female, for you are all one in Christ Jesus" (3:28). The Apostle Paul takes this one step further by saying, "In humility value others above yourself, not looking to your own interests but each of you to the interests of the others" (Philippians 2:3–4). Scripture exhorts us to reject all the ways the world tries to rank human worth, such as gender, ethnicity, race, education, or socioeconomic standing. As followers of Jesus we are to view others not only as equals but as people who should be honored. Thus, as God's kingdom people, when we humbly look to the interests of others, and truly value their needs, it brings healing and justice to those people and places.

This week for our practice I want us to prayerfully notice who around us is marginalized or vulnerable. For example, it could be migrants crossing the border or people of color who experience racial inequality and injustice—among many other groups the Lord could bring to mind. Once you have prayerfully noticed the person or people the Lord is drawing your attention to, then ask, "What causes this marginalization or vulnerability? And what can I do about it?" Next, spend a few minutes praying and ask the Lord to give you one tangible way to practically love the person or group of people he brings to mind. Keep in mind, it could be doing something practical for someone or it might be educating yourself, so you start to gain a better understanding of why a group of people is marginalized. Once you have an idea, write it below and make a plan for how you can accomplish these next steps of self-giving love.

Start each day with this simple prayer:

> Lord, help me to notice those around me who are marginalized or vulnerable and to see them as your beloved children. This week, give me a tangible way to extend love to someone or to a group of people who are marginalized or vulnerable.

Take a minute to pray: "Lord, help me to notice
those around me who are marginalized or vulnerable and to see them as your beloved children.
This week, give me a tangible way to extend love
to someone who is marginalized or vulnerable."
Now look for ways you can act on this prayer.

Day 2
Esther's Brave Next Step

Read Esther 5:1–8.

1. According to Esther 4:16, 5:1 and 4, how did Esther prepare
   before she went to see the king? What do you think she was
   feeling when she walked into the inner court to see the king?

2. Read James 2:20–26. Fill in the blank below for how James
   might have included Esther in this passage.

   In the same way, was not even Esther the queen considered
   righteous for what she did when she

   _____ .

   How does Esther's story illustrate the truth that faith and
   action should work together?

It's important to read James 2 within the context of all of Scripture, so we properly understand the relationship between faith and action. Other verses make it clear that we are saved by faith alone through grace alone and not by anything that we do or don't do (Romans 3:23–24; Ephesians 2:8–9). So, when James talked about our faith resulting in action, he wasn't saying we should act to earn something from God. Rather, he was saying that our faith should lead us to action as a response to who God is and what God has done for us.

3. It's a rare thing for us, as contemporary women in stable countries, to have our lives threatened for doing what God asks us to do. But make no mistake, God does ask us to do things we might not wish to do. Things that could threaten our status, our comfortable lifestyles, even our easy faith. Much like the message from Mordecai to Esther, God can interrupt our lives and invite us to take on a task for him. Are there areas where you've been sensing God's nudge to take action? Take a moment and pray for the Lord to reveal areas in which he's asking you to do something. Write down what the Lord brings to mind. How will you do this? What concerns do you have?

What strikes me about Esther is that she followed through. She started with a brave and bold statement in chapter 4 that she would go to the king and if she perished, she perished. And then just two short verses later we learn that three days passed and she did what she said she would do.

I wonder what she thought about over those three days as she contemplated her meeting with the king. So many things could go wrong. If it was me, I would have started playing through all the scenarios—spending the most time on the worst ones, of course.

The author of Esther doesn't tell us what Esther thought about over those three days of waiting and preparing. However, the author does tell us that she fasted along with the community. This means she was most certainly praying. And so, while we don't know what she was thinking, we do know she was directing her thoughts toward heaven and gathering strength from God. Going without food drove her to intentionally seek God. She showed up to the king not weak with hunger, but strong with faith.

She followed through. It's a great lesson for us. There are times when we know the right next thing to do—it feels brave and bold in the moment. We can see ourselves following through in obedience. And then a few days pass and it can start to feel like just a crazy idea, foolish even. If we aren't careful, we can talk ourselves right out of obedience. I know I can. I've done it before. We can learn a few things from Esther to help us follow through. First, invite others to be on the journey with you and declare your intentions to them. Second, seek God in prayer. And finally, go. Follow Esther's lead and bravely do what you have declared you will do.

4. Esther approached the king's throne uncertain of how he would respond to her. Read Hebrews 4:16. Fill in the table on the next page noting the contrast between how Esther approached Xerxes's throne and how we are invited to approach God's throne.

Xerxes's Throne	God's Throne

When have you experienced the truths in Hebrews 4:16? Is there a place in your life where you need to experience these truths right now? Consider sharing this with your group and inviting them to pray with you.

"The prayers and fasting of God's people, joined with trust in God, are no guarantee our lives will be spared. We've lost count of the numbers of faithful, trusting believers who have been martyred for their faith. Hadassah could have easily been one more name on the roster of forgotten martyrs."

—Carolyn Custis James[1]

PRACTICE REMINDER

Take a minute to pray: "Lord, help me to notice those around me who are marginalized or vulnerable and to see them as your beloved children. This week, give me a tangible way to extend love to someone who is marginalized or vulnerable." Now look for ways you can act on this prayer.

Day 3
Pride's Downfall

Read Esther 5:9–14.

5. According to these verses, what are some of the things you notice about Haman's character?

6. Read Proverbs 16:18. How does this sum up Haman's character and his coming future? Who are some modern-day people who seem to have Haman's character? How does this verse encourage you or discourage you regarding this person?

"Pride gets no pleasure out of having something, only out of having more of it than the next man."

—C. S. Lewis[2]

Pride is sneaky and dangerous. It's been said to be the root from which all sin grows. We have to be vigilant to keep pride at bay by staying in continual dependence upon the Lord. If we let pride go unchecked, we could wind up where Haman found himself. His unbridled pride turned into malice. Theologian and author Warren W. Wiersbe said, "Malice is that deep-seated hatred that brings delight if our enemy suffers and pain if our enemy succeeds. Malice can never forgive; it must always take revenge. Malice has a good memory for hurts and a bad memory for kindnesses."[3]

7. According to Ephesians 4:31–32, what is the antidote to malice? How does extending kindness to someone make it impossible to have malice in your heart for them?

8. Read Colossians 3:8–12. According to this passage and the other passages we've read in this lesson, where do you think the seeds of malice come from? Are there any "seeds" in your heart that could grow into malice? What are they? Confess them to the Lord and ask him to help you practically root them out. What steps will you take to root out these seeds this week?

Take a minute to pray: "Lord, help me to notice
those around me who are marginalized or vulnerable and to see them as your beloved children.
This week, give me a tangible way to extend love
to someone who is marginalized or vulnerable."
Now look for ways you can act on this prayer.

Day 4
Waiting

Read Esther 6.

Esther, for one reason or another, felt led to wait before she told
the king her request. And it's a good thing she did. Sometimes
timing is everything—and sometimes waiting sets up the exact
right timing. Unfortunately, waiting feels counterintuitive for
most of us. Living in a hyper-fast world has only compounded
our impatience with waiting on pretty much everything. If the
website doesn't load immediately, I shut it down and try again. If
my text doesn't get a quick response, I wonder what's gone wrong.
If I know there is news coming, I can't get it out of my head as I
wait and wonder. But God isn't concerned with our time schedule or desire for immediate results. He is working things out on
his schedule—which is always the right one. Psalm 27:14 gives us
some excellent advice: "Wait for the LORD; be strong and take
heart and wait for the LORD." When we wait for the Lord, we
allow him to set the stage for the right next steps to unfold.

9. King Xerxes can't sleep. What happened as a result (verses
   1–2)? Thinking about Esther's fasting, praying, and waiting, how do you think the events in these two verses reveal
   God's providence? How will this help support Esther's plea

to save the Jews? (See week 1 page 20 for a definition of *providence*.)

10. Have you ever had an experience where you felt led to wait before you made a big move or decision? What happened? If you were able to learn the why behind the wait, how did it reveal God's providential hand in your life?

Haman's pride was still in overdrive. When the king asked what should be done for someone the king wanted to honor, Haman was certain he was the honoree. Haman exhibits all the classic traits of a narcissist—he is self-absorbed, believes he deserves special treatment and honor, and lacks empathy for those around him. He really can't see past himself, but that's about to change.

11. What was Haman's recommendation for how honor should be bestowed (verses 6–10)? Based on what you know of Haman, how do you think he felt when he found out the king wanted to honor Mordecai?

There are many things I wonder about in this passage. For starters, how can King Xerxes support an edict to kill every Jew in the province one minute and then turn around and bestow honor on a Jew the next? I also wonder how Haman, riddled with malice and rage, was physically able to utter the words over and over, "This is what is done for the man the king delights to honor!" I even wonder about the people living in the city. What in the world did they think? The Jews were sentenced to die, and now a Jewish man was being publicly honored with all this pomp and circumstance. It must have been disturbing. And, finally, I wonder about Mordecai. How did he feel about all this? We don't get answers in the text, but this whole debacle points to the reality that King Xerxes is unstable and unpredictable. And this is the man that Esther stood before. Only God could make anything good come of this.

Read Esther 7:1–6.

For the third time, King Xerxes asked Esther what her petition and request were, and for the third time, he told her he would give her up to half the kingdom. This offer wasn't meant to be taken literally. It simply meant that Xerxes would be generous to her, and it was his way of inviting her to tell him plainly what she wanted. It's also worth noting that up to this point neither Xerxes nor Haman had any idea she was a Jew.

Esther then made her bold request to the king and asked him to spare her and her people's lives.

"The LORD detests all the proud of heart. Be sure of this: They will not go unpunished." (Proverbs 16:5)

12. Read and compare Esther 7:4 with 3:13. What do you notice? How do you think her use of the words "I and my people" let the king know what her true identity was?

13. How does the king respond in verse 5? Why do you think he had to ask who had done this? What does this tell you about how much of an impression the edict made on him? How exactly did Esther identify and describe Haman (verse 6)?

"Although lost in English translation, the king's fury is effectively communicated in the Hebrew words, which sound like a machine-gun fire when pronounced aloud. His honor is offended that someone would attempt injury to his queen and her people."

—Karen H. Jobes[4]

14. Compare 1 Peter 5:8 with Esther 7:6. Who is our adversary and enemy? How was Haman serving this adversary's purposes?

Jesus said, "The thief comes only to steal and kill and destroy; I have come that they may have life, and have it to the full" (John 10:10). I love these words because they remind me that while the enemy is real, he does not win. Haman may be serving this enemy by bringing death and destruction, but his plans do not succeed because God is in control. And Jesus, through his life, death, and resurrection, ushers in the ultimate victory. Through faith in him we are given life, and abundant life at that. The enemy may be prowling around ready to pounce at a moment's notice, but our God is bigger and we can rest in the truth that he has won the battle against our adversary.

15. Where do you currently see and experience our adversary and enemy prowling in your life, your home, your work, your country, or our world? According to 1 Peter 5:8–9 (and other Scriptures), what are some of the ways we can resist him?

Take a minute to pray: "Lord, help me to notice those around me who are marginalized or vulnerable and to see them as your beloved children. This week, give me a tangible way to extend love to someone who is marginalized or vulnerable." Now look for ways you can act on this prayer.

Day 5
Defeating the Adversary

Read Esther 7:7–10.

This is the pivotal moment in Esther's story. The pent-up tension can get lost on us since we know how the story ends, but Esther had no idea what would happen. She had to stare down the crossroads of obedience to God knowing that if she followed where he was leading, there was no certain outcome. She and her people could have died. It had to be truly scary. I think it was all this emotion raging in her body that made her finally point her finger toward Haman and blurt, "It's him! This vile man is the enemy here. He wants to kill me and my people!" (my interpretation).

The king's rage is palpable. But what will he do next? He's been unpredictable at best through this whole story. What those moments must have been like for Esther, we can only imagine.

16. Describe the scene in the banquet hall. What do you think Esther felt after she finally pointed out Haman? What did Haman do? How did the king interpret Haman's actions?

～❋～

"What a paradox! Haman had been furious because a Jewish man wouldn't bow down to him, and now Haman was prostrate before a Jewish woman, begging for his life!"

—Warren W. Wiersbe[5]

·······

17. Swift justice was executed. What happened to Haman? While the justice in this instance is not something we would wish on our worst enemies, where do you long for God's justice in your life or in our world? What could that look like?

It's ok to think the book of Esther is funny at times, because it is meant to be. It's written in an ancient style that mimics irony and comedy with reversals of fortune that drive the narrative forward. Most of these reversals center around Haman, who sets an elaborate scheme to destroy Mordecai, but continually gets caught in his own trap. He builds a pole intended to impale Mordecai and winds up impaled on the pole instead. He initiates a decree that would kill and plunder the Jews, and he winds up dead with all his wealth taken. He thinks he will be honored in a royal parade, but he has to parade through the streets honoring Mordecai instead. Mordecai even winds up with Haman's job in the end.

While all of these reversals are ironic in nature, they reveal something more important. Pride is not honored in God's eyes and eventually he will set things right. In this case the prideful man, Haman, is completely removed from the story and the humble man, Mordecai, is elevated to a position of influence. It's a good lesson for us that pride doesn't win in the end.

Jesus, the one true king who had every right to demand worship and honor, is a prime example of what it looks like to embrace the opposite of pride and have a servant's heart and posture instead. He summed it up by saying: "You know that the rulers in this world lord it over their people, and officials flaunt their authority over those under them. But among you it will be different. Whoever wants to be a leader among you must be your servant, and whoever wants to be first among you must be the slave of everyone else. For even the Son of Man came not to be served but to serve others and to give his life as a ransom for many" (Mark 10:42–45 NLT).

18. Esther had been clearly called by God. What were some of the things God allowed in her life that made her the perfect person to save the Jews? What was the result of her bravery and obedience?

What could have been the result if she decided not to obediently follow God's invitation for her? What sacrifices did she have to make?

Make no mistake, Esther isn't the only one called by God to enact his good purposes; you are also called by God to do good work which he has prepared in advance for you to do (Ephesians 2:10). Like Esther, you have been created with beautiful intentionality. You are uniquely made and gifted and have been placed in this time and space of history "for such a time as this." I believe we face many "for such a time as this" crossroads moments in our lives—some small and some large. My prayer as I write this is that

God would help you see your crossroads moments clearly and discern how he is inviting you to follow him. I'm also praying that you will find courage to say a brave and bold yes to his invitation. Obedience to God, while often costly, is always worth it.

We are often lulled into thinking obedience to God isn't that big of a deal, but it is. The enemy might suggest our calling isn't that important, but it is. And we may begin to think the path is too hard or unnecessary, but it isn't. If we truly believe God is who he says he is and will do what he says he will do, then we need to follow him, no matter the cost or where he leads us. Esther is a great example to us in this way. Obedience cost her dearly. Even though she was afraid for her very life and had no idea how her story would end, she bravely and obediently followed what she believed God was asking her to do. May you do the same.

19. Earlier in this lesson, I invited you to ask the Lord to reveal areas where he's asking you to take action. Take some time to again ask God if he might be leading you to take the next step of obedience in one of those areas. Is something holding you back? Why? What are you afraid might happen if you do this thing? What encouragement can you take from Esther's story this week to help you overcome these fears?

20. Looking back at your answer to question 3 on page 55, has the Holy Spirit led you to change your answer at all? If so, why might that be? If your answer hasn't changed, how is the Lord encouraging you and inviting you to follow him? Spend some time praying and journaling right now, asking the Lord for courage and strength to follow him in obedience. Then commit to take the next step of obedience that he's leading you to. Share this with your group for accountability and encouragement.

PRACTICE REFLECTION

1. Think back to this week's practice activity. Were you able
   to show love in a practical way to someone who is marginalized or vulnerable? If so, how?

2. What was this activity like for you? Did it reveal anything
   to you about God and his heart for the marginalized and
   vulnerable?

THE GREAT REVERSAL

Day 1
Practice—Holy Feasting

In ten short chapters of Esther we read about nine different banquets. These large and small meals guide the book. You might recall that our story began with an extravagant six-month bender intended to show off and celebrate the king's power and wealth. Then our story ends with a much different meal, a holy feast intended to remind the Jews of what God had done and how, against all odds, he had saved them. These two feasts stand in stark contrast to each other. One honors the fleeting power of a man and the other the everlasting provision of our God.

This whole concept of holy feasting is striking to me. As I've reflected on it, I've come to realize I'm not very good at it. Actually, *we* aren't very good at it. Aside from Thanksgiving, I'm not sure we, as a society, much less as a Christian community, set aside times to feast and be intentionally thankful. Don't get me wrong. We're great at having a big meal, but feasting is different. Feasting is planned and prepared for. It's slower and more deliberate. Most importantly, holy feasting carries intention as we celebrate why we feast instead of just mindlessly eating until we fall asleep on the sofa.

Holy feasting is a spiritual discipline. Scripture recounts meal after meal as examples to us. For example: the Passover (Exodus 12; Luke 22:7–20), where God spared his people from death, was a commemorative meal Jesus shared with his disciples and is still widely practiced by devout Jews today; or the Feast of Pentecost also known as the Festival of Weeks (Deuteronomy 16:10–12; Acts 2:1) which celebrated the grain harvest where people brought the first of their grain as an offering to the Lord. These meals teach us how to celebrate with the savoring of good food and drink while we intentionally recount and recall God's faithfulness. Holy feasting gives us space to share a meal and a story of a time when God showed up. These intentional meals remind our souls of the faithfulness of God, while at the same time encouraging our brothers and sisters who sit at the table with us. These meals become sacred places.

With this in mind, I want us to practice holy feasting this week. I know you only have a week, so let me give you some easy steps to make this happen. First, spend some time prayerfully reflecting back over the last few weeks to notice where you have seen God's providential hand guiding your life. Ask yourself: Has there been an answered prayer? A coincidence that was really God's guiding hand? A circumstance that only he could orchestrate? A miraculous intervention that left me awestruck? A place I've seen God's abundance and provision, even in the valley? Whether small or big, notice and record below what the Lord has done.

Next, pray about the person you should invite to a meal or coffee to share these stories with. When someone comes to mind, reach out to them right away and get something on the calendar. Write your plan below.

When you meet together, share what you've written down.

Since you only have a week to do this, you may need to be creative about what your feasting looks like, but I want to encourage you to make it special. Have the cupcake. Get the pasta. Drink the fun drink. And as you do, slow down and savor it. Let the abundance of flavors remind you of the abundance of our God.

If it feels weird, you have permission to blame me. You can say something like: "So, I'm doing this Bible study, and I'm supposed to share with someone how I've been seeing the Lord show up in my life. I've prayed about it, and the Lord brought you to mind. I'd love to share some of these things with you, and I would love to hear what he is doing in your life too." See that wasn't so weird, was it?

It's ok to feast a little. Even if you are experiencing extremely difficult times, I want to encourage you to try to do this practice. God has never left you or forsaken you and perhaps the discipline of feasting and recounting God's providence in your life is exactly what your soul needs.

PRACTICE REMINDER

If you haven't done so already, remember to set
aside time to reflect on God's providence in your
life and then schedule a time to tell these stories
to a friend . . . while feasting, of course.

Day 2
The Bigger Picture

Read Esther 8:1–14.

As we learned in the last lesson, the story of Esther is full of reversals. You may recall that Haman was impaled on the exact pole meant for Mordecai, Haman's entire estate was then given over to Mordecai, and finally Haman's post as second in command was also awarded to Mordecai. But not all the difficulties were reversed. The edict to kill the Jews still stood—despite Esther pointing it out to the king. It appeared that while Mordecai and Esther might be saved in spite of this edict, the clock was still ticking toward the dreadful day that was intended to annihilate the Jewish people. Esther had already risked her life once on the issue, and the king, who responded with killing Haman, seemed satisfied that he had done enough. But the Jewish people's lives were still in grave danger. Thus her calling had yet to be fulfilled, so Esther once again faced a crossroads.

1. What did Esther do? How did the king respond? How do
   you think she felt when she went before the king this time
   as compared to Esther 5:1–2?

2. According to Esther 1:19 and Esther 8:8, what cannot happen to a decree issued by the king? What was the solution
   Esther suggested (8:11)?

3. Read and compare Esther 3:13 with Esther 8:11. What do
   you notice about the similarities between the edicts? What
   is different?

4. Consider how this illustrates the larger narrative of sin and
   death in Scripture. What was the decree God gave the first
   man and woman in the garden (Genesis 2:16–17)? How did
   the death and resurrection of Jesus satisfy this decree on
   our behalf (Romans 5:18–19; 6:23; 2 Corinthians 5:21)?

A civil war was authorized as the only solution for the Jews' sur-
vival. This is disturbing to us as it seems to highlight violence
as the solution. However, we need to remember that this is a
descriptive verse about what happened and not a prescriptive or
timeless truth about how we should do things now. In fact, Jesus
invites us into a different way of solving our problems.

5. Read and summarize Jesus's words in Matthew 5:43–48. How do Jesus's words stand in stark contrast to what happened in Esther?

Our best defensive tactic is to go on the prayer offensive. What might that look like in your life? (Keep in mind that we are not called to move back into any kind of abusive or dangerous relationship.)

Pray and ask the Lord if you need to love someone differently than you are right now. How do you think the Lord is inviting you to do this? Make a plan and share it with someone for accountability, encouragement, and prayer.

If you haven't done so already, remember to set aside time to reflect on God's providence in your life and then schedule a time to tell these stories to a friend . . . while feasting, of course.

Day 3
The Tables Are Turned

Read Esther 8:15–17.

The book of Esther seems like it is fast-moving because it is short and packed with action, but if you slow down and read closely you will notice that events don't happen as quickly as they appear to. For starters, ten years passed between the banishment of Vashti (Esther 1) and the second edict that saved God's people (Esther 8). Ten years. That's how long it took to get Esther in place and prepared for her "for such a time as this" moment. Time also passes slower than it seems between the first and second edicts. The Jews had to live under threat and promise of death for a full two months and ten days before the second edict was issued that gave them the right to protect themselves. We struggle to wait a few days for test results. Can you imagine what it must have been like to open your eyes each morning, for seventy mornings, knowing death was looming on the near horizon?

It's a good reminder for us that God is always working and acting but he is on his own schedule, not ours. Ten years feels long. So does two plus months. But even if it feels slow to us, we can't forget that God is moving. He never forgot the Jewish people, he never forgot Esther, and he hasn't forgotten you. This is real life and real life takes time. Maybe you've been waiting on God for years. If so, can I encourage you? Don't give up. He sees you. He loves you. He will meet your needs and answer your prayers. If not here, then fully and finally in our eternal home. Keep waiting on him. He's preparing your "for such a time as this" moments.

6. How did the Jews respond to the new edict? How does this compare to how they responded to the first edict (Esther 4:3)?

The Jews feasted and celebrated because they were given the right to defend themselves. There was still a war coming, and there was no guarantee people wouldn't lose their lives. Yet they didn't grieve—they celebrated. They took the long view of victory. They knew their God would prevail, and thus they would prevail.

What a testimony to us. We need to take the long view of victory. Life is a battle. We have an enemy. We get no guarantees for this life, and yet, the long view tells us there will be an ultimate victory because of Jesus. We can rest and trust in this, and we too can choose to celebrate even though a war is bearing down on us.

7. Reflecting back on your life, when have you experienced a reversal where a season of mourning, fasting, weeping, or wailing turned into a season of joy, gladness, feasting, or celebration? What truths about God do you wish you embraced more fully as you waited in that uncertain season? If you could go back and live that season over, is there anything you would do differently in light of these truths?

8. What are some of the uncertainties of life that are currently weighing on you? How could you take the long view, like the Jews did, and embrace the truths of God to turn your fears into trust? Spend some time writing a prayer below, confessing these fears to God and then embracing the truths he offers you.

Read Esther 9:1–19.

The day Haman declared as the day of death had finally arrived. Although Haman was dead, his legacy of hate lived on as many Persians attacked God's people. But the day turned out to be nothing like the day Haman had plotted. Instead of a power-less slaughtering, the Jews were emboldened and prepared. They were a minority, but they had God on their side. And a minority plus God always makes the majority. They could not and would not be defeated.

9. How does Esther 9:1–3 describe what happened? What are some of the reasons the Jews had the upper hand?

All ten sons of Haman, who are listed by name, were killed and then impaled on poles for public display. This feels barbaric to us, and it is, but it's a practice of ancient warfare. It was important to remove the entire family line so that no one could come back to seek revenge. This harkens back to the battle between the Amalekites and the Jews when King Saul spared King Agag from death (see week 2, day 2 on page 39). King Agag preserved a hate-filled remnant of the Amalekite line which eventually led to this attempt at revenge toward the Jews. Killing every son meant the entire line was now wiped out and the Amalekites could no longer be a threat to the Jews.

10. How many people lost their lives as a result of Haman's hateful edict (verses 6–10, 15–16)?

11. Thinking of recent world events and your own life, how do you see the evil plans of wayward people being carried out today (either large scale or small scale)? Do you see God in the midst of these trials? If so, how? How do you reconcile these terrible events with God still being a good God who is in control?

One of the most evil atrocities that has ever happened was the brutal murder of Jesus himself. It seems that if God ever had the power to stop something from happening (which he does), he could have stopped this. It was brutal, cruel, and senseless, and it happened to Jesus, God's very own Son. Yet God, in the greatest reversal in history, took this most ultimate evil and turned it into the most ultimate good. Through Jesus's death and resurrection, we are restored into relationship with our creator and given life everlasting. This doesn't mean that Jesus's death wasn't evil. It was. But God . . . (these are some of my favorite words in Scripture and life). But God . . . can take these things and somehow redeem them and use them. He doesn't discount or ignore evil. He hates it, and we should too. The long view tells us that evil has been defeated. There will come a day when evil will be no more, and all that is broken will be made right. Until that day comes, we are called to remember truth, bring it to bear where we can, and live in light of the long view.

12. Read and summarize the following Scriptures. How do these verses encourage you to hold on to the long view of what our future holds? How do they encourage you today?

Psalm 46:9–10

Revelation 21:3–5

1 Corinthians 15:51–58

PRACTICE REMINDER

If you haven't done so already, remember to set aside time to reflect on God's providence in your life and then schedule a time to tell these stories to a friend . . . while feasting, of course.

Day 4
The Feast of Purim

Read Esther 9:20–32.

13. According to 9:21–22, how often and why were the Jews to celebrate? What were some of the things to be included in the observation of Purim? Why do you think this was?

14. According to 9:28, how many years was the Feast of Purim to be celebrated? Why? How would celebrating the feast ensure that the truths of the story would live on?

Every year Jews, from young to old, still gather to celebrate the Feast of Purim as a joyous way to remember and recount the faithfulness of God. One of the aspects of the celebration is the public reading of the book of Esther. Whenever Haman's name is spoken, it is tradition for children to twirl *graggers* (noisemakers) and for adults to stamp their feet to symbolically eradicate his name. The celebration also traditionally starts with a fast and ends with a feast to mimic the story of Esther.

15. What traditions (religious or nonreligious) do you celebrate with your family or friends? What meaning do these traditions have for you? What impact do they have on your relationships with the people you celebrate with?

Part of the purpose of celebrations is to come together and connect with people in our circles, but, like the Feast of Purim, they can also have deeper meaning. While Christians don't typically participate in this celebration, we do have other celebrations and traditions that help us remember and recount God's story.

One of my favorite traditions that we celebrate at my church is the season of Lent. It's the forty days that lead up to Easter. We start with an Ash Wednesday service where we contemplate our frailty, our brokenness, and our need for Jesus. During the next forty days, I often fast from something. Sometimes it's from a particular food or drink and other times it's from an activity, such as social media. The intent is, just as it is with any fast, to draw me closer to Jesus and remind me that he is better than any of these comforts or activities. The best part is Easter morning. My heart is ready to celebrate his resurrection and what it means for me and the entire world. And then, the icing on the cake is the Easter feast we have later in the day. There is something extra sweet and celebratory about savoring a feast after a season of fasting.

16. What are some of the annual Christian celebrations or tra-
    ditions you participate in? How do these remind you of the
    story of God's faithfulness? How do you keep these tradi-
    tions from becoming mindless rituals?

17. Celebrations are a great way not only to thank God for what
    he has done but also to help us remember his faithfulness.
    Is there a tradition you would like to begin celebrating?
    Perhaps a God-engineered reversal in your life (see question
    7 on page 78 if you need a reminder of those times), a cele-
    bration based on something in Scripture, a day to simply
    say thank you for spring, or a day to remind yourself of
    what God has promised he will do. How might you start
    this tradition? How do you think it would be meaningful?

PRACTICE REMINDER

If you haven't done so already, remember to set aside time to reflect on God's providence in your life and then schedule a time to tell these stories to a friend . . . while feasting, of course.

Day 5
Mordecai's Greatness

Read Esther 10.

The book of Esther can be summarized as a story of God's providential protection over his people through irony and reversal. Chapter 10 puts an exclamation point on this reversal for Mordecai.

18. Think through Mordecai's story in the book of Esther. List some of the reversals that happened in the book. (Here are a few verses to get you started: compare 3:1 with 10:3; 3:10 with 8:2; and 5:14 with 7:9–10.) How do these reveal God's providence? (As a reminder you can find the definition of *providence* in week 1 on page 20.)

19. Think through Esther's role in this story. List some of the things that made her the perfect person for the task God called her to.

20. How does the story of Esther specifically encourage you? How does it specifically challenge you?

I love the story of Esther. When I've studied Esther with friends and one of us needs courage or is getting ready to step out in faith, we often say to one another, "Perhaps this is your 'for such a time as this' moment." This little shorthand draws me back to Esther's story and makes me think of her standing at the crossroads and choosing boldness and bravery. And with these words, I draw my shoulders back a little, take a deep resolved breath, and think, "Perhaps it is." Esther gives me courage to be brave and take risks. I hope she does the same for you. Maybe you can adopt this little shorthand with some of your Bible study friends as a way to encourage them when they are stepping out in faith too.

21. What next step do you feel the Lord is inviting you to take as a result of what you have learned or been challenged by through Esther's story? Share this with your group for prayer and accountability.

PRACTICE REFLECTION

1. Were you able to have a celebratory meal and share how you have seen God working in your life? If so, what happened? If not, when do you have it scheduled?

2. What was this activity like for you? Did it reveal anything to you about God or his people?

RESISTING
AND RUNNING

Day 1
Practice—The Daily Examen

This week we shift from Esther, who responded with bold bravery when faced with her crossroads, to Jonah, who had an entirely different response. Every time I study Jonah one thing always pops up early in the discussions: Jonah may not have liked what God was asking him to do, but at least he knew exactly what his assignment was. Jonah had the advantage of a clear, most likely audible voice telling him exactly where to go and what to do. Have you ever thought, "If God would just give me a clear sign—like write something on the wall or speak in an audible voice—then I would do whatever he called me to." I have. I used to think that a lot when I was younger in my faith journey.

I remember fretting over making just the right God-honoring decision at just the right time. Which college, which roommate, which event, which job . . . good night, I even fretted over what to wear sometimes. I often got myself so locked up in decision-making that I became paralyzed by indecision. I would cry out, "Please God, just tell me what to do." But the longer I've walked with God, the more I've come to know that he rarely gives those near audible directives . . . especially about what I should wear. Instead, he reveals his will in other ways—through his Word, his people, circumstances, opportunities, and prayer, to name a few.

As we cultivate a daily relationship with him, many of these smaller decisions just flow naturally out of that place. But when a bigger decision comes our way, it's good to take some time to discern how he's leading.

One of the ways we can start to discern God's leading is through noticing his presence and prompting throughout the day. By making space to thoughtfully notice and reflect on God's movement, we can start to see God's leading and directing. This practice of noticing is a spiritual discipline Christians have been doing for a very long time called "the daily examen."

An examen usually happens at the end of the day, just before you go to bed, but it can be helpful at other times during the day too. It is an intentional time to notice and reflect upon the last twenty-four hours and to ask God to guide you in the next twenty-four hours. This week I'd like you to take some time each day to do the examen. It doesn't take long, maybe five to ten minutes, and the benefits will be well worth the effort. To do this, copy the questions under "The Daily Examen" below into a notebook and place it somewhere you won't miss it—like next to your bed or the coffee maker. If you are able, do it right now. Then, each day, at your chosen time, reflect on the examen questions and make notes of your answers. Do this each day for the entire week.

God may not speak in an audible voice to us, but he is present and moving. He is leading and guiding. I pray this activity will help you start to notice and follow him more.

The Daily Examen

- When did I feel close to God over the last twenty-four hours, or when did I notice his presence? Why?

- When did I feel distant from God? Why?

- When did I experience the fruit of the Spirit: love, joy, peace, patience, kindness, goodness, faithfulness, gentleness, and self-control?

- When did I experience the opposite of the fruit of the Spirit? Why?

- How do I want to intentionally seek the Lord throughout my next twenty-four hours? (Spend a few minutes praying for his help in these areas.)

PRACTICE REMINDER

If you haven't already, take five to ten minutes to reflect on and answer "The Daily Examen" questions listed on pages 89–90 in this book.

Day 2
Reasonable Reluctance

The Book of Jonah
Author: Unknown
Date Written: Jonah was a prophet during the reign of King Jeroboam II (793–753 BC), which places the date of writing near this date.
Purpose: Jonah was written to remind us of God's loving concern for all people regardless of what they have done. Jonah also teaches us that when we repent, we do so before a gracious and merciful God.

Jonah and Esther are similar in that God called both individuals to save an entire group of people. They differ in that Esther was called to help facilitate the salvation of God's people, her people—a people she loves. Jonah was called to help bring salvation to his enemy—a group of people who had been brutally terrorizing others, including his people, for decades.

We study Jonah and Esther together because they were both called to do something monumental that changed history and because they had very different responses to God's call. Esther, as we saw, acted with boldness and bravery. Jonah, as we will see, acted with reluctance. On the surface, I would much rather have someone consider me to be like Esther than Jonah, but as we dig in, we will see it's much more nuanced and complicated than simply bravery versus cowardice.

Let's start with a little backstory on Jonah to place him in history so we can begin to understand. Jonah lived a few hundred years before Esther. He was identified as a prophet of God who lived during the reign of one of Israel's wicked kings, Jeroboam II (2 Kings 14:23–25). A prophet was God's mouthpiece, speaking directly what the Lord said. They often spoke words and did acts that called God's people to repentance, warned them of judgment, or looked forward to Jesus. Being a prophet was hard and often unpopular—especially when they called people to repentance. I don't think prophets often had a lot of friends.

The prophet Jonah, however, was given a different task than all the other prophets. He was called not to the Jews but to the Assyrians, who lived in the city of Nineveh. The Assyrians were a brutal enemy to God's people and had been for the last hundred years. They were also proud of themselves, so they recorded everything through pictorial and written accounts, which means we have detailed records of just how terrible they really were. According to theologian and author James Bruckner, "Records brag of live dismemberments, often leaving one hand so they could shake it before the person died. They made parades of heads, requiring friends of the deceased to carry them on elevated poles. They boasted of their practice of stretching live prisoners with ropes so they could be skinned alive."[1] Lovely. The Assyrians were the worst of the worst, and God called Jonah to be a foreign missionary to go to save these murderous heathens from God's punishment. Think of it like being called to go preach a message of salvation and forgiveness to Hitler, Stalin, or Kim Jong-il and their sympathizers. No, thank you.

Jonah is often called the reluctant prophet and for good reason. First, his calling was dangerous; there was a high possibility of death going into the Assyrians' camp. Second, going meant he would need to overcome his hatred for a group of people he believed deserved God's wrath instead of his mercy. Finally, if he did go and survive, what would God's people think of him when he returned? Would he ever be accepted back into the community? Any way you look at it, the costs of this mission were incredibly high and long term. His reluctance is understandable.

Unlike in the book of Esther, God is front and center in this story. He is no longer the unseen main character: he is the main character. He is the one who calls, rebukes, leads, and teaches. As you will see, we have a lot to learn from Jonah's interactions with God.

Similar to Esther's story, the book of Jonah is a narrative with a story arc. Again, it is helpful for us to read the whole story before we dive into its parts. While you may be familiar with the story of Jonah (most of us have heard about the man who got stuck in the belly of the huge fish and lived to tell about it), I'd like to encourage you to read the whole book with fresh eyes. The story is about much more than being swallowed alive . . . and surviving. In fact, the whole fish incident is just a few verses out of the whole book. Jonah is only four short chapters and will take just a few minutes to read.

Read the entire book of Jonah. Write down anything that stands out to you or any questions you may have.

If you haven't already, take five to ten minutes to reflect on and answer "The Daily Examen" questions listed on pages 89–90 in this book.

Day 3
Running

Read 2 Kings 14:23–27 (printed below).

1. Second Kings 14:23–27 provides some context for what was happening in Jonah's day with the nation of Israel. Circle all the ways that Israel's king, Jeroboam II, is described. Put a square around Jonah's name and then write out what you learn about Jonah. What do you think it was like for Jonah to be a prophet under King Jeroboam?

> Jeroboam II . . . reigned in Samaria forty-one years. He did what was evil in the LORD's sight. He refused to turn from the sins that Jeroboam son of Nebat had led Israel to commit. Jeroboam II recovered the territories of Israel between Lebo-hamath and the Dead Sea, just as the LORD, the God of Israel, had promised through Jonah son of Amittai, the prophet from Gath-hepher.
>
> For the LORD saw the bitter suffering of everyone in Israel, and that there was no one in Israel, slave or free, to help them. And because the LORD had not said he would blot out the name of Israel completely, he used Jeroboam II, the son of Jehoash, to save them. (NLT)

Read Jonah 1:1–3.

2. Jonah was told, "Go to the great city of Nineveh and preach against it, because its wickedness has come up before me." How did Jonah respond? Considering what you read about Nineveh in day 2, why do you think he responded this way? Why do you think this task was so much worse than being a prophet to Jeroboam?

"Jonah wants a God of his own making, a God who simply smites the bad people, for instance, the wicked Ninevites and blesses the good people, for instance, Jonah and his countrymen."

—Timothy Keller²

3. The Ninevites represented a group of people who had committed such heinous cruelty against others that Jonah believed they deserved God's just punishment. Who are some people you would characterize as "Ninevites" in our world today? How do you think you would feel if God asked you to go preach to them so that they might be changed and find forgiveness for their offenses? (To keep group discussion on topic, please do not answer out loud who you might characterize as modern-day Ninevites. Please focus on the "how you would feel" part of this question.)

4. Read Psalm 139:7–10, a Scripture passage Jonah would have been familiar with. What does this passage say about our ability to run from God? How do you feel about this verse—comforted, frustrated, or something else? Why?

Scholars don't know exactly where Tarshish is, but they do know it's in the opposite direction from Nineveh. This means Jonah didn't just avoid doing what God told him to do by employing delay tactics, creating busywork to distract himself, or just ignoring what God said (which, by the way, are common things we all do when we don't want to obey God). No, he was much more bold in his choice. He actually chose to do the exact opposite of what God told him to do. Jonah resisted God so deliberately it's almost as if he looked him in the eye and said, "I don't care what you want me to do; I'm not doing it."

5. Think back over your life. Was there a time when you knew the Lord was asking you to do something, but you resisted him? What happened?

6. Pray and ask the Lord to help you notice if there is any area where you are running from or resisting him now. If something comes to mind, why do you think you are running or resisting? Pray about this openly with God, confess your struggle to him, and ask him to help you follow his plan. If you feel comfortable, enlist your group to pray for you as you seek to follow God.

It's only fair that I also take an honest look at my own life to see how I'm running from or resisting God, so I'm going to be vulnerable and honest with you. As I prayed during the writing of this book, God showed me that I've been resisting his call to practice being still with him each day. Psalm 46:10 is his invitation for me to sit in stillness in his presence with no agenda as a way of surrender. Instead, I keep moving. I keep working. I keep doing, which is really my way of telling God I don't trust him. I believe that if I choose to be still, then things won't get done. So I read my Bible, pray, and move. Instead, I should read, pray, and be still. I say I trust him, but I'm not acting like I do. You have my permission to ask me how it's going when you see me. Be gentle with me, though; I have a little Jonah in me.

Jonah's reaction is very different from Esther's. Admittedly, we don't have all the details of her being brought to the palace and if she even had a choice, but once she was there, surely she could have resisted through other means. She didn't, though. She seemed resolved from the beginning that she would be an active and willing participant in God's story unfolding before her—even when she didn't know what was coming next.

7. As you reflect on Esther's story as compared to what you know of the start of Jonah's story, what do you think was similar about their callings? What seems different? Do you think one calling took more courage than the other? Explain why.

PRACTICE REMINDER

If you haven't already, take five to ten minutes to reflect on and answer "The Daily Examen" questions listed on pages 89–90 in this book.

Day 4
Storms

Read Jonah 1:4–10.

8. What did the Lord do in verse 4? Why do you think he did this?

9. What did the sailors do? What was Jonah doing? How do you think he was able to sleep amid all that was happening?

10. Jonah's actions caused chaos. Reflect on a time when the choices you made caused chaos in your life or the lives of others. What happened? Did the chaos help move you back toward the Lord? Why or why not?

It's important to note that not all storms come into our lives as a direct result of our disobedience, and not all disobedience leads directly to storms. Yet there are times when we make choices to be willfully disobedient, as Jonah did, and as a result, storms and chaos will enter into our lives. And sometimes others get caught in the storms we've stirred up. These storms are never meant to punish us but to lovingly draw us back to God (Proverbs 3:11–12). In many ways, they are God's grace upon us. If Jonah had arrived in Tarshish he may have felt better for a bit, but reality would have set in that he had willfully forsaken his calling and his God. His heart would have longed for restoration. Of course, God would take him back, but that specific calling may not have been available anymore as God may have used another method to fulfill his plans. Through the storm, God got Jonah's attention and invited him once more into obedience and relationship.

11. Who else experienced the storms (verse 5)? What does this tell you about other reasons why storms may come into our lives? Did the storm feel differently to them than it did to Jonah? What storms have you experienced in your life and in our world that were a result of others' choices?

The sailors had prayed to their various gods, and the captain had called on Jonah to pray to his God. Nothing was working, and the storm was getting worse. Everyone was afraid for their lives. So, in their desperation, they cast lots to see if they could discover who was behind all this chaos. The casting of lots was a common practice used for decision-making in Israel and other nations in the ancient Near East (Acts 1:21–26). In this case, God allowed the lots to reveal that Jonah was the guilty party.

Once the sailors knew Jonah was the reason for the storm, they asked him a series of five questions. These questions seem a little redundant and cumbersome to us—after all, the ship was threatening to break apart as the storm raged on—but these questions were an attempt to solve the why of the storm and hopefully make it stop. To the sailors and in accordance with their worldview, each of these questions could reveal the identity of a potential offended deity. By asking Jonah's occupation, hometown, country, and race, they were looking for clues that would reveal a specific deity. If they could pinpoint the offended deity, then maybe they could figure out how to appease this deity and stop the storm.[3]

12. How did Jonah respond to the sailors' questions? Do you think he responded to the question, "What kind of work do you do?" If so, what do you think he said?

13. These questions were meant to expose the gods (more accurately, the false gods) that were worshipped in their day. Today we can also inappropriately worship "false gods" when we depend on people or things for our pleasure, identity, or security instead of God. What are some of the false gods people turn to today? How do you see people leaning on these false gods to make them feel significant or to solve problems? How do these gods distract us from the one true God?

14. From the list of false gods you brainstormed in the last
    question, what are the things you are tempted to turn to
    instead of God? If you feel like these things have misplaced
    God in some way, confess this to him and ask God to help
    you take steps to put him back in his proper place. Write
    down an idea or two for how you will do this.

"Shallow Christian identities explain why professing Christians
can be racists and greedy materialists, addicted to beauty and
pleasure, or filled with anxiety and prone to overwork. All this
comes because it is not Christ's love but the world's power,
approval, comfort, and control that are the real roots of our
self-identity."

—Timothy Keller[4]

•••••••

PRACTICE REMINDER

If you haven't already, take five to ten minutes to reflect on and answer "The Daily Examen" questions listed on pages 89–90 in this book.

Day 5
Read Jonah 1:11–16.

The storm picked up. It was already deadly violent, and here we learn it continued to get worse. In desperation the terrified sailors asked Jonah what they should do to him. They knew that since he was the cause of the supernatural storm, he was the only one who could appeal to God to fix it. At this point in the story, Jonah was still steadfastly resistant to God. In many ways he was willing to choose death over obedience. His response essentially said he'd rather drown in the raging sea than go to Nineveh.

15. What did Jonah tell the sailors to do? How did Jonah accept responsibility for what was happening? Do you think there was another way? If so, what might that have been?

"Did they have to throw him in? Could Jonah not jump in himself? After all, he had brought such devastation to the ship and its crew already—surely it was a step too far to implicate them all in manslaughter? Perhaps it was, but . . . death was only the logical outcome because Jonah insisted on continuing on the road that led there."

—Paul Mackrell[5]

In one final effort to fix the problem and save all the people on board, the sailors tried to turn back to shore and row with all their might to get out of the storm, but it didn't work. In fact, the storm got even stronger. This is the second time we are told that the already violent storm's rage intensified. They had tried everything they could think of to fix the problem in their own strength; now it was time to do what must be done.

16. What did the sailors decide must be done? How did they address God? Why do you think this was significant? What did it indicate might be happening in their hearts?

Notice that when the sailors cried out to the Lord, they were praying. These pagan men, who believed in multiple false gods, now turned to the one true God. This is a significant irony that reveals deep truth about our God. Even though Jonah fled his call to preach to the pagan nation of Nineveh, he wound up being a witness for God, even in his disobedience, to these pagan sailors.

17. What happened as soon as Jonah went into the sea? We don't really know, but imagine you are the sailors in this intense situation and then Jonah goes into the sea. What do you think this immediate calm was like for them? What did the sailors do next? Why do you think they did this?

18. Read and summarize Job 42:2 and Romans 8:28. List some of the ways the truths of these verses are reflected in Jonah 1.

19. Think of a recent storm in your life. How did this storm help you, like the sailors, turn to the one true God? What happened? What did you learn about God through this trial?

PRACTICE REFLECTION

1. Looking back over your notes for this week's practice of the examen, do you notice any patterns or themes? If so, what could that mean for you moving forward?

2. Based on the examen, what do you think the Lord is inviting you to change, embrace, or confess?

3. Take a few minutes to journal about your experience and how you desire to move forward with God into the next week.

PRAISE FROM THE DEPTHS

Day 1
Practice—Giving Away Something Useful

Jonah chapter 2 took place almost entirely inside the belly of a huge fish. That alone is unbelievable, but let's not get distracted by the whole fish thing yet—we'll get there. For now, I want us to focus on one line of the prayer that Jonah offered while he was in the belly of this fish. He said, "Those who cling to worthless idols turn away from God's love for them" (Jonah 2:8).

I've been pondering these words and how true they are for me. When I cling to anything other than God, I actually turn away from his love. Often my turning from his love isn't intentional, but I miss him due to being distracted by something else. Our world gives us lots of distractions to cling to: time, stuff, relationships, schedules, image, health, and the list goes on and on. None of these are bad in and of themselves. In fact, a schedule is super helpful for me, but when I start clinging to it, it gets elevated to idol status and distracts me from what God is inviting me to instead.

This week I want us to do a simple activity to help us loosen our grip on one potential idol I think we all wrestle with: stuff. Whether we have a lot or a little, when we start getting clingy with our things, we can miss God. So this week, I want us to give some of these things away. No, I don't want you to Marie Kondo your closet and say goodbye to things that no longer give you joy; I actually want you to say goodbye to a few things that *still* give you joy.

To do this we will give away at least one thing that is still useful to us but that we think will bless another. Start this practice with prayer, asking the Lord to bring someone and something to mind. Then make a plan to gift this thing to them as a blessing to them. When you get an idea, run with it.

I'm not going to lie—this may seem easy, but it isn't. At least it wasn't for me when I did it a few years ago. Here's what happened: I had a younger friend who had recently started baking. She was making pies almost every day and was contemplating starting a baking business. The Lord brought her and my set of pie weights to mind. For you non-bakers, pie weights are these little ceramic balls that you put in the pie crust when you bake it. They keep the heat even and the crust flat. They aren't a big thing, but they're really nice when you're making a pie. I really liked my pie weights, but this was the thing the Lord brought to mind. So I packaged up my pie weights and brought them to her. I felt a little silly when I gave them to her and told her how helpful they were to me and that I thought she might enjoy them. She thanked me, and while I think she liked them, I actually have no idea what she really thought. It's a high possibility she thought my used pie weights and I were weird. I do hope they blessed her, but truthfully it was more about me and my heart than the gift or how she received it.

The whole act of praying and then acting to give something away was incredibly meaningful to my relationship with the Lord. It still serves as a great reminder that I do not need everything I have, but what I really need is him. To this day, I still wish I had a set of pie weights. I will not replace them, though, because Jesus is better than pie weights. I know that sounds silly, but the pie weights are an object lesson that reminds me that he is better than anything and everything I own. Giving up my pie weights helped me loosen my grip on stuff so I could tighten my grip on him. This is the theme of our lesson this week.

I'll look forward to hearing how the Lord teaches you through this activity. Oh, and if you have a set of pie weights, maybe I could borrow them sometime?

- Take a few minutes to pray and ask the Lord to bring a person and possession to mind. Write down any ideas that come to mind.

- Choose one of the ideas above and make a plan for how you will give them your gift before the end of the week. Write it below.

PRACTICE REMINDER

Have you said goodbye to something that
still gives you joy? If not, take some time to
ponder the someone and the something,
then make a plan.

Day 2
A Really Big Fish

This week, we will read the firsthand account of Jonah's har-rowing near-death experience. He nearly drowned and was swal-lowed by a huge fish. At the end of himself, he finally seeks God in prayer while inside the fish and was then vomited (yes, there's actually a biblical Hebrew word for *vomit*) onto dry land. To put it clearly, Jonah was saved because he was eaten by a ginormous, slimy fish. Only God can think up these things.

This lesson covers a few themes that are joined by the com-mon thread of learning to cling to and surrender to God and his will for us. Clinging to God is essential. As his chosen ones, it's the only way we can avoid some of the pitfalls we see Jonah succumb to.

Read Jonah 1:17.

This one verse has been a tripping point for generations. I mean, how could a fish swallow a whole man? And even if there was a fish big enough to swallow a man, how could the man survive it? It truly is unbelievable. Was Jonah real and could this really happen?

It's important to answer this question because having a firm foundation in our trust in God, the truth of his Word, and his providential care for us is necessary before we can surrender to him and his will for us.

It's interesting to notice that Scripture never refers to the fish that swallowed Jonah as a whale. Where did that idea come from? It's probably because whales are the biggest sea creature we know of, but it's entirely possible that whatever type of fish swallowed Jonah is now extinct.

1. Read Matthew 12:38–41. What did Jesus say about Jonah? How do Jesus's words about Jonah indicate that he believed the story of Jonah?

"The 'sign of Jonah' is the expression used by Jesus (Matt. 12:39–41) to refer to Jonah's (and his own) three days and three nights in the belly of the fish/tomb. . . . The wonder of the sign is that a *place that ought to have been a place of death becomes a place of deliverance and life.*"

—James Bruckner[1]

2. Read the following verses, then draw a line to match each verse with the related event.

Events	Scripture References
Sarah at 90 and Abraham at 100 had a child together	Matthew 1:18
God parted the Red Sea for the Israelites to walk through	Genesis 21:1–5
Mary, a virgin, conceived Jesus through the Holy Spirit	Mark 16:6
Jesus fed 5,000 people with five loaves and two fish	Exodus 14:21–22
Jesus rose from the dead	Matthew 14:19–21

Do you struggle to believe any of these events? Why or why not? How do they impact what you believe is possible in Jonah's story?

Here's what I find amazing. There was a huge storm that would normally drive big fish down. But instead of disappearing into the depths of a vast sea, this one fish was led by God to be just where it needed to be at precisely the right moment to save Jonah. Just as in the book of Esther, God moved at the exact moment he was needed, not a moment too soon or a moment too late. In Esther, God's provision and rescue took the form of providence, as we studied in weeks 1 and 2. At this point in the story of Jonah, providence was still happening, but God made sure we could not miss that he was the one orchestrating it.

I think it's also important to note that both of the circumstances Jonah and Esther found themselves in were terrible. Jonah was drowning in a raging storm. If you've ever been sucked under by the ocean, you know a small bit of the disorientation and panic he must have experienced. And it was in this moment of almost certain death that the fish swooped in to save him. And Esther was one of hundreds of women taken and trafficked to a man who couldn't have cared less for her wellbeing, at least until he got to know her. And once he did get to know her, she was able to go before him to make her audacious request. It's hard to imagine the gravity of their situations. But it's important to notice their responses. Because while we will never find ourselves in their exact circumstances, we may find ourselves in some pretty terrible ones. How will we respond in those crucible moments—with the faith of Esther or the resistance of Jonah?

As a reminder, *providence* is God's active and intimate involvement in sustaining our world and providing for the needs of people, especially those who follow him in faith, even when we don't clearly see it.

....

3. Jonah was in the belly of the fish for three days and three nights. Write down or draw what you imagine this might have been like (consider the space, smells, sounds, temperature, lighting, etc.).

4. While sinking in the churning waters, do you think Jonah understood that the giant fish was a provision of rescue? How do you think he might have been feeling once he was inside the fish's belly?

5. Take a moment to prayerfully consider and write down some of the ways the Lord has providentially rescued you. How are these provisions just as miraculous as what you've read about in the verses in today's lesson?

Here's another interesting fact about Jonah's fish. Jonah 1:17 uses the gender neutral/masculine form for the belly of the fish, and then in Jonah 2:1 it switches to the feminine form for the belly of the fish, which would be understood as the fish's womb. This has scholars puzzled. Why would the author of Jonah switch the fish from neutral/masculine to feminine? Some think it's simply a scribal error, and while that could be true, I think there's more to it than that. I think the author was suggesting that there was a reversal in the works. The sailors and Jonah assumed that the role of the fish was to punish and consume Jonah. But God had something else in mind. Instead of the fish eating Jonah, it provided for and protected him like a mother's womb until Jonah could be delivered to his place of purpose. This is significant to me because, just like Jonah, I've had storms come into my life that initially felt like they might drown me, but instead God arranged my deliverance from the storm. I can look back on the big fish of deliverance and see it as God's grace to me instead of something intended to harm me.

6. Has there been a time in your life where you had a perspective shift about something that, like Jonah's fish, initially seemed like it might harm you and instead it led to your protection and deliverance? Describe what happened. Spend a few minutes thanking the Lord for his grace to you in that situation.

PRACTICE REMINDER

Have you said goodbye to something that *still* gives you joy? If not, take some time to ponder the someone and the something, then make a plan.

Day 3
In Distress

Read Jonah 1:17–2:2.

While we don't know exactly what Jonah was thinking and feeling as he waited inside the fish, we do know he prayed. His prayer echoed the Psalms he grew up memorizing. In this moment of distress Jonah clung to what he knew to be true of God as he recited parts of the Psalms. Jonah shows us that knowing God's Word is an essential aspect to being able to surrender to God. God's Word is the steadying truth that helps us navigate the uncertain and hard times.

Jonah's prayer in the belly of the fish echoes and alludes to the following psalms: 18, 30, 31, 42, 69, 77, 86, 88, and 116. And if you keep digging you will find even more references. It's a good reminder that God's Word can help us in times of difficulty, just like it did Jonah.

7. Read Psalms 18:6 and 86:13. How do these verses echo Jonah 2:2? Why do you think it was important for Jonah to be able to draw upon these truths in that moment?

8. Knowing God's Word can be essential when we are really struggling, but his Word does more than just encourage us in challenging situations. Write down what the following verses say about Scripture and how knowing it can help us.

Psalm 119:11

Psalm 119:104–105

John 8:31–32

2 Timothy 3:16–17

Hebrews 4:12

9. Have you had an experience where a truth from God's Word did what one of the verses above describes? If so, what happened? If not, why do you think that is? What are some practical ways you could move forward in trusting in God's Word to do what it says it will do?

10. What are some ways you strive to keep God's truth present in your heart and mind? Share these with the group to get ideas for how you can continue to be intentional with knowing God's Word. As the group shares, write down some new ideas to try.

11. Take a few minutes to look up a verse that encourages you. Write it on a sticky note or note card. Place it somewhere you will see it so you can start memorizing it this week. (Here are some ideas to get you started: Romans 8:28; Romans 8:38–39; Psalm 27:1; Proverbs 3:5–6; James 4:7; Philippians 4:6–7; and Ephesians 2:10.)

There are a lot of ways to memorize Scripture, but they all take intentionality. The intentional effort is worth it because when you need truth and encouragement, you often need it right away. If Jonah didn't have these truths embedded into his heart, his fears might have taken over even more than they already had. Here's a suggestion for one way to start memorizing: Take the verse you've written out from question 11 and place it on your bathroom mirror. Read and practice it while you brush your teeth every day until we finish our study. Then choose another verse and start again. Go back and review the verses as you learn new ones, so you don't forget the previous ones.

Have you said goodbye to something that
still gives you joy? If not, take some time to
ponder the someone and the something,
then make a plan.

Day 4
Downward Spiral of Disobedience

Read Jonah 2:2–8.

It has been noted by many who study Jonah that, to this point, he has been depicted as going down. He went down to Joppa (1:3), then he went down to the ship (the NIV does not reflect this but the original Hebrew language does), then he went down below the deck of the ship (1:5), and finally he went down into the depths (2:3). The author intended for us to see the downward spiral that Jonah had embarked on through his disobedience.

As we will see, disobedience isn't the only reason trials come our way. No matter the reason, though, these trials should drive us to God not away from him. It's in these hard moments where we can make a powerful move of surrender to God.

12. How did Jonah describe what happened as he was going down into the depths? Who did he say was responsible (verse 3)? Why do you think he would do this to Jonah?

13. Read Hebrews 12:6, 10–11. What do these verses say God does for those he loves? Why does he do this? According to these verses, why did God discipline Jonah?

"God's mercy reached Jonah in the depths of the sea. It also reached Nineveh in the depths of its wickedness. Neither one was deserving."
—Paul Mackrell[2]

14. Have you ever been on a downward spiral caused by disobedience? What happened to finally pull you out of that situation? How do you think this was God's discipline in your life? What fruit ultimately came out of this situation?

15. It's important to note that not all hard circumstances happen as a result of our disobedience. According to the following verses, what are some other reasons trials may enter our lives? What additional reasons can you think of?

John 9:1–3

Romans 8:20–22

1 Peter 5:8–9

In Jonah 2:6, Jonah declared, "But you, LORD my God, brought my life up from the pit."

And with this, the downward spiral seemed to stop.

He then goes on to state that "those who cling to worthless idols turn away from God's love for them" (verse 8). Idols, much like the false gods discussed in the previous lesson, are people or objects that we lean on or elevate in such a way that they take the place of God in our lives.

16. Jonah doesn't seem to include himself in verse 8. However, what idols might Jonah have been clinging to and not even realized it? Who might he have been thinking about? What idols were they clinging to?

While we can't overlook that all Christians struggle to keep God first in their life, in the truest sense, this verse is talking about idols that ultimately keep people from knowing God altogether.

17. Think through some of your friends and family who don't know the Lord. What are the things that you think keep them from knowing Jesus? How do these people or things act like idols in their life? How are these things ultimately worthless (John 3:16–18)? Take a moment to pray for each of these people by name, asking the Lord to reveal himself to them. Ask the Lord how you might or might not be part of that revelation.

Day 5
Finally on Dry Land

Read Jonah 2:9–10.

Jonah's stubborn disobedience to God's call led to an absolute nightmare. But in these verses, he seemed to humble himself enough to turn back to God. As we'll see in the next few chapters, it wasn't a complete change of heart, but it was a start.

A lot of journeys God asks us to take can feel scary since we can't see the whole picture or end results. It's like we're walking along on our journey and suddenly the path dips just beyond the crossroads, and all we can see is a forest ahead that swallows the path in darkness. When this happens, fear of the unknown can immobilize us. We may not run away from God as Jonah did, but we certainly aren't boldly responding to God's call like Esther did either. Jonah teaches us that God's invitation is to a journey that starts in our hearts. As we remember the truth of who God is and offer him the praise he deserves, we can trust him enough to take the first big step of surrender toward obedience. And with each step we take, we find that while the whole path doesn't get illuminated, God does give us enough light to take the next step.

18. What did Jonah say he would do in verse 9? How was this a big change from everything he had done so far?

19. Recalling where Jonah was and how long he had been there, how do you think Jonah could say he would do something with shouts of grateful praise? How does this encourage you to worship—give shouts of grateful praise—even in your darkest moments? Have you ever been able to do this? What was the result?

Jonah had not fully arrived on his faith journey, but he committed to take a step of obedience. I think it would have been amazing if Jonah had a complete change of heart toward the brutal Ninevites. But he didn't, and honestly, that feels more like real life. Heart change is a process, often a long process. But this small step, which happened as Jonah surrendered in his heart, led the Lord to command the fish to vomit him on dry ground. Covered in muck and weary from the journey, Jonah gets up and takes the first step of obedience.

"Faith in Yahweh is never as simple as pure obedience versus pure rebellion. Jonah helps us see the complexity of faith. He returns to his piety and worship of the true God of heaven, sea, and dry land. At the same time he maintains reservations of protest against God's intended way in the world with the violent Ninevites."

—James Bruckner[3]

20. Pray and ask the Lord if there is a step, even a small step, of obedience that he is asking you to take. What is it? How will you do this?

21. Is there anything holding you back from taking this step of obedience? Considering Jonah and where he had been, how does his journey comfort you or challenge you to move forward in spite of whatever you feel is holding you back?

22. Look back through this week's daily sessions and consider all the ways Jonah shifted in his heart posture and thinking. How is the Lord inviting you to follow in Jonah's footsteps? How will you do this?

PRACTICE REFLECTION

1. How has your practice of giving something away this week impacted you?

2. Has it helped you recognize some things you might be cling-ing to? If so, what are they and how might they be holding you back from following where the Lord is leading you?

   Pray and ask the Lord to give you some practical ways you can loosen your grip on anything that detracts from him. Write down any ideas he gives you and commit to doing these things.

JONAH'S OBEDIENCE AND GOD'S COMPASSION

Day 1
Practice—Sharing Good News

Jonah was finally back on dry land. I'm guessing he sat on the shore feeling exhausted and amazed, yet defeated. There was nothing left for him to do, except what God had asked him to do—and what he had agreed to do just moments before, while he was still in the belly of the fish. He'd barely had a chance to catch his breath or dry off before "the word of the LORD came to Jonah a second time: 'Go to the great city of Nineveh and proclaim to it the message I give you'" (Jonah 3:1–2).

God was telling Jonah to *go* and *tell*. *Go* to Nineveh and *tell* them what I say to you. Easy and yet so difficult. Jonah would need to overcome not only his hatred and prejudice but also his fear. He had every reason to be nervous for the task ahead of him. Why would these irreverent people who were so bent on violence listen to a man sent by God?

Truthfully, they may not have listened. They may have chased him out of town. They may have done terrible things to him. Those were all very real possibilities. But the end results didn't truly matter; the results were in God's hands. What mattered was Jonah's obedience. Would he *go* and *tell*?

We are faced with a similar yet very different predicament today. As believers, we are called to *go* and *tell* people about Jesus. Jesus himself commissioned us to do this good work (Matthew 28:18–20) and the book of Romans echoes this by reminding us that people need to know about Jesus, but "how can they hear about him unless someone tells them?" (Romans 10:14 NLT). As followers of Jesus, our calling to tell others about him is crystal clear. Unlike Jonah, though, we probably won't be called to wander through a hostile town heralding the good news of Jesus and calling people to repentance. That doesn't mean sharing the good news is easy, though. Sometimes we are called to share Jesus with people who might be considered hostile, but just like with Jonah, the results are not up to us. The only thing we are responsible for is sharing about Jesus when we have the opportunity.

Even when people around us are receptive to hearing about Jesus, it can still feel scary to share. We start to wonder: What if we don't know how to answer their questions? What if they think we're weird, like those soapbox street corner preachers, and start to avoid us? What do we say? How do we even begin? We have a lot of questions. Some are legitimate, but most just serve as barriers to keep us from sharing the good news.

One of the best ways to help us overcome these fears is to remember just how good the news about Jesus really is. To help you with this, think through these questions. How has Jesus been good news for you? What has he done in your life? What is he doing in your life right now? How has he cared and provided for, rescued, brought freedom to, transformed, or renewed you? When we remember these truths about Jesus, it makes it easier to share him with others. He is, after all, life-changing good news for now and eternity.

For our practice this week, I want to challenge us to *go* and *tell* at least one person who doesn't know Jesus yet about the hope-filled good news. To do this, start with a simple prayer every day, asking the Lord to bring someone across your path you can bless with the good news of Jesus. Then keep your eyes open for a divine appointment. Sharing the good news could take many forms. It might be a story you share from your life. It might be an act of generosity that allows you to explain that you are being generous because Jesus has been so generous to you. Don't limit how God wants you to share the good news.

PRACTICE REMINDER

Remember to pray, "Lord, bring someone into my path today I can bless with the good news of Jesus." Then be on the lookout for divine appointments to share the good news.

Day 2
Second Chances

Read Jonah 3:1–3.

Jonah had just been vomited onto dry land. Seriously, ew. I cannot even imagine—exhausted, hungry, and now covered in the muck of fish vomit. We can be sure this whole experience of running from God has been both exhausting and traumatic for him. Thankfully all we will ever have to do is imagine how awful this whole fish ordeal must have been. There's very little chance we will wind up in the same circumstances Jonah found himself in. However, many of us do know all too well the exhaustion of running from God.

God spoke to Jonah a second time (3:1) and this time he was ready to listen and obey. The Hebrew expression translated as "Jonah . . . went" (3:3) implies Jonah's immediate obedience. Nineveh was about 500 miles from Jerusalem, so depending on where the fish deposited Jonah, he had quite the walk or donkey ride ahead of him.

1. Fill in the chart on the next page comparing Jonah 1:1–2 with 3:1–2.

Passage	Similar	Different
Jonah 1:1–2		
Jonah 3:1–2		

Jonah was given a second chance to obey God and, thankfully, it's not just Jonah who gets second chances. Another famous passage is when Peter, a disciple of Jesus, was given a second chance after he failed. It's good to know our God is a God of second chances because we all need them. Let's look at Peter's life to see what more we can learn about the second chances we are given.

"When God calls a person to a specific mission, the task and the journey do not always make sense. God is, nonetheless, often persistent in such calling. Moses repeatedly argued with Yahweh concerning the Exodus (Ex. 3:11–4:17). . . . Jeremiah struggled with Yahweh concerning his call (Jer. 20:7–9). Jonah was never convinced by Yahweh's argument about the need to transform Nineveh's wickedness."

—James Bruckner[1]

2. Read Luke 22:54–62. This passage takes place after Jesus was arrested and just before he was crucified. How did Peter fail? How many times did he do it? When he realized what he had done, how did he respond? How do you think Peter felt at the realization of failure?

3. Read John 21:15–19. This passage takes place after Jesus's resurrection. Peter and Jesus were sitting on the shore of the Sea of Galilee, having just had breakfast together. What questions did Jesus ask Peter? How many times did he ask him these questions? After Peter's reply to each question, what did Jesus say next? What did Jesus say at the end of verse 19? How do you think this made Peter feel?

Like Peter, we've probably all been in places where we've been tempted to hide our faith for some reason. This kind of denial can lead us to shy away from telling or showing others who Jesus is, and as we saw in our practice section, we are all called to share Jesus with the people around us.

It's really important to note that while these passages talk about specific failures, they are not making a statement about our salvation. Our salvation is not dependent upon our actions; it is solely dependent upon our faith in Jesus. Scripture after Scripture confirms this truth (John 3:16; Romans 3:23–24; 8:38–39; and Ephesians 2:8–9 to name a few). We will fail, but we will not lose our salvation.

4. Both Jonah and Peter received a second chance. What did God ask each of them to do (Jonah 3:2; John 21:17, 19)? What is similar between these second chances?

5. How does it encourage you that our God is a God who gives second chances? Are there times when you think he doesn't give a second chance? If so, why do you think that is?

6. Have you ever said no—or hesitated for a long time—to do something you believe God asked you to do? What happened? Do you think it is possible to get a second chance at this thing? Why or why not? If you think it's not possible, because maybe the situation is passed or some other reason, how can you commit to responding differently in the future?

If you've never talked to the Lord about this incident, spend some time in prayer now telling him how you feel about saying no to him. As you do, remember that you are extravagantly loved by him, and your salvation is secure in him. If you are able, tell him you are sorry. As you do, imagine him as the loving Father he is and allow your heart to know he receives you with open arms, embraces you, reminds you that he loves you, and invites you to follow his lead again.

I'm so grateful that our God is a God of second chances, third chances, even one hundredth chances or more. In my own faith journey, I falter often. I choose my way over his way more than I'd like to admit. Just this morning he revealed a place where I was operating out of fear instead of trust. And this fear was leading me to try to control a situation that I had no real control over. I've done this type of thing more that I can count. And each time I recognize I'm doing this and turn back to him in trust, the response is the same—a welcome embrace and full forgiveness. Our God is a loving and forgiving God. He still absolutely wants us to follow his lead the first time, but when we mess up, he is ready and willing to help us get back on track again. What a good God we serve!

7. Spend some time writing out a prayer to the Lord, telling him how you feel about following him and how you feel about doing whatever he asks you to do. If you are hesitant, tell him why. If you want to make a bold commitment, do so. If your heart feels hardened about this, ask him to help you there. Wherever you are, offer this to the Lord.

Remember to pray, "Lord, bring someone into my path today I can bless with the good news of Jesus." Then be on the lookout for divine appointments to share the good news.

Day 3
Proclaiming the Truth

Read Jonah 3:3–5.

8. Write down the message word for word that Jonah was to proclaim to the Ninevites. Considering the situation and what you know about Jonah and the Ninevites, what do you think about Jonah's brief message?

After all Jonah had been through, the message God gave him seems pretty lackluster. While the possibility of God's mercy was embedded in the message, it still feels like there should be some overt call to repentance or at least a mention of God, yet there isn't. It's an example to me that God's ways are not my ways. It's also a reminder that I'm called to follow him and his ways. Thus, I need to be careful to avoid putting my own spin on things. Since God doesn't speak audibly to me like he did to Jonah, that means I need to be intentional to try to stay in step with the Holy Spirit so I have the best shot at following where God is leading.

9. Given what you know of Nineveh, what are some possibilities for how the Ninevites could have reacted toward Jonah's message? We know how Jonah's story ends, but it's important to remember that Jonah didn't. If you were Jonah, what would you have been afraid might happen?

10. Read Romans 10:14–15. As you read these verses replace "Ninevites" for "they." And replace the word "someone" with "Jonah." How does this passage apply to Jonah? Read the passage again and now insert the name of someone you know who does not know Jesus yet. This time, you are the "someone." How does this passage encourage and exhort you regarding your practice of sharing the good news this week? Take a moment to pray for the person you inserted into the verse and ask the Lord for an opportunity to share the good news with them.

I came to know Jesus when I was a thirteen-year-old at camp. I wasn't raised in a Christian home and had hardly ever been to church. And yet, I knew I was deeply broken and needed help. So when the camp counselor shared the good news one night around the campfire, I didn't need to hear it twice. I prayed right there on the spot, and everything about my life changed from that point on.

Here's the thing I have to remember: they had to tell me the good news. I didn't know who Jesus was, I had no idea what the Bible said, and I had no idea how to find the Savior I needed. I was looking for something and thankfully, because of their faithfulness that night, they introduced me to Jesus. I shudder to think how I would have tried to fill the void and help myself if no one ever shared the truth with me. We share because people need to hear. Without hearing, they won't know. It feels risky, but I'm grateful someone took that risk.

11. How did you come to know Jesus? If someone shared the gospel with you, what happened? How does this reinforce the truths in Romans 10:14–15 for you?

12. Read 1 Corinthians 3:6–7. What does this say about what our responsibility is and what God's responsibility is? How does this encourage you in sharing Jesus with others?

PRACTICE REMINDER

Remember to pray, "Lord, bring someone into
my path today I can bless with the good news
of Jesus." Then be on the lookout for divine
appointments to share the good news.

Day 4
A Drastic Response

Read Jonah 3:5–10.

13. How did the Ninevites respond to Jonah and God's mes-
    sage? Why is this surprising?

It's interesting to note how far the king was willing to go. He
decreed everyone should fast, and not just a normal fast from
food, but also drink. And not just people, but also animals. The
text seems to indicate that this went on for forty days, since Jonah
said the city would be overthrown in that time. It's unclear why
the king went to such extremes and included the animals, but it
seems he was trying to show God just how repentant he and the
people were.

Can you imagine what this must have been like? People, including children, starving and dehydrated. Animals starving and
dehydrated. I imagine the sounds from the hungry animals alone
were disconcerting. If I don't feed my dogs right on time they
start to grumble and complain with increasing volume as the
minutes tick by. Can you imagine what herds of hungry cattle

sounded like? That is, until they got too weak to cry out anymore. And then I imagine fear set in. If the people of Nineveh lost their cattle to starvation, how would they survive once the fast was over? This sacrificial fast took a lot of faith. They had to believe that the fast, as incredibly uncomfortable as it was, could perhaps save them in the long run.

14. Read Esther 4:3 and recall what the Jews were experiencing under King Xerxes's reign. How was the response of the Ninevites similar to how the Jews responded? How was it different? What were they both hoping would happen as a result of their actions?

Fasting is recorded in many places in Scripture, both in the Old and New Testaments, and is often linked to prayer. While fasting is not commanded for believers, we see examples of Jesus (Matthew 4:2) and the early church (Acts 13:2–3; 14:23) fasting. Jesus fasted as he entered a season of temptation and trials, and the early church fasted before they made big decisions. Both examples are about the person's heart being more focused and aligned with God. The fasting we do, as children of God, is much different than the fasting the Ninevites did. They were trying to get something from God as they showed him they were willing to change their ways if he would save them. Today we can fast for many reasons—repentance, discernment, deliverance, healing for ourselves or others—but no matter the reason we fast, it is to draw near to the God who has already saved us. We cannot earn anything from God when we fast, but our fasting can help our hearts become more tender to him and aware of his leading.

15. Have you ever fasted from food or anything else for spiritual reasons? (Recall we did this in our first week's practice section.) If so, why and what happened? What did you notice about your relationship with the Lord as a result of the fast? If you have never fasted, what might be a reason to fast, and what would you fast from?

16. Read Jonah 3:8 below. Circle the two things the king told everyone to do.

    Let everyone call urgently on God. Let them give up their evil ways and their violence.

    If they had called on God but kept doing evil, what might that have said about them? If they had stopped doing evil but didn't call on God, what might that have said about them? Why do you think doing both of these things mattered?

17. Read James 2:14–17. How did the actions of the Ninevites mimic James's exhortation to us? Is there any place you feel like you need to couple faith with action today? How will you do this?

Day 5
Relenting

Read Jonah 3:9–10.

The Ninevite king boldly declared his hope for the city's fasting and repentance by saying, "Who knows? God may yet relent and with compassion turn from his fierce anger so that we will not perish" (verse 9).

18. What did God do and why? How do you think the Ninevites felt about this? The text doesn't tell us, but what do you think the Ninevites did once they realized they were saved?

The concept of God relenting is tricky. On the one hand, we read Scriptures that make it clear God does not change his mind (Numbers 23:19; James 1:17), and then, on the other hand, we read accounts like this that say he can change his mind. How do we reconcile this? Most theologians reconcile this with the understanding that God does not change his mind in respect to the big picture plan of salvation for the world, yet there are times when he can and will make a choice to do something different when it doesn't interfere with the big picture plan. This is why it's important for us to boldly make our requests to God, because he seems to make these choices when we have asked him to do so.

19. Read the following verses about prayer and write what stands out to you most.

John 15:7

James 1:5

James 5:16

1 John 5:14

According to these verses, how do our prayers make a difference? How does this encourage you in your prayer life?

The act of God relenting and having compassion on the Ninevites was still left to God's sole discretion. He could have chosen a different response. In fact, he had every right to destroy the city as he said he would.

20. Read 2 Samuel 12:16–18, 21–23. (Note: These passages are about King David's sin of sleeping with Uriah's wife, Bathsheba, and then having Uriah murdered to cover his sin. The child referenced is the result of David's affair.) Compare 2 Samuel 12:22 with Jonah 3:9 and note the similarity between these verses. Does God always relent? How do you think he decides?

It's hard for us to understand why some requests are answered and others aren't. One of my dear friends lost her baby boy after fifty-six short days. We prayed hard for this precious baby. Not just me but our whole church went to their knees on behalf of this family and their child. There were moments when it felt like God was answering us and other moments when a doctor's report made it feel hopeless. Ultimately, God chose to answer our requests for healing with an irrevocable no when this sweet boy passed away. We all grieved, but none more than his parents. And yet, we all, including his parents, found comfort as we turned back to God and reminded ourselves of who he is and what was ultimately coming.

21. Read Revelation 21:1–5. What are some of the truths this passage tells us about what our future holds?

22. What are some requests you have prayed for that haven't
    been answered? How does remembering what our ultimate
    future is help you deal with these unanswered requests?

23. Read Romans 3:23–24. How does remembering what Jesus
    did for us through his death and resurrection and thinking
    about our ultimate future encourage you in your calling to
    share the hope of Jesus with others?

PRACTICE REFLECTION

1. Were you able to share the good news with someone this week? If so, what happened? If not, what held you back?

2. What was this practice like for you? Did it reveal anything to you about you, God, or his people?

OUR NINEVITES

Day 1
Practice—Praying for Our Enemies

Jonah was mad, really mad. I can hardly blame him.

He'd finally surrendered to God. He went to the city of Nineveh, a place where torture was sport and evil was relished. He preached an abrupt message, which led everyone to repent and beg God for mercy. It's truly unbelievable. A lot about Jonah is unbelievable, but this is exceptional. It would be like going into a Nazi military camp and all of a sudden Hitler and every soldier turned from their evil ways . . . and God forgave them!

It makes me wonder: How do people who are blinded by evil finally see things differently? The only answer is God. What happened in the city of Nineveh was an absolute miracle, and it made Jonah mad. I imagine he thought that these people didn't deserve grace. They didn't deserve a second chance. They should have paid for what they did. They should have suffered the same kind of cruelty they inflicted, and then maybe he would have been ready to talk about some grace. The scales of justice were seriously out of balance on this one.

Yet God seems perfectly fine with the scales of justice being off. Somehow he is a God who is one-hundred-percent full of grace and one-hundred-percent full of justice—at the exact same time. Jonah didn't get it. We don't either, but we have an advantage over Jonah that helps us. We get to see all this from the other side of the cross. It is at the cross, where Jesus died for us while we were still sinners, that we see God's grace and mercy as he forgives all our offenses toward him. We didn't deserve it; we still don't. It is at this same cross that we see our God carry out justice as the full penalty of sin is paid for through death, his death. Full of grace and full of justice. This is our God.

But it's still hard on us, isn't it? I mean, there are people out there we struggle to believe are deserving of God's grace. We can make a list right now: traffickers of young girls, instigators of genocide, warmongers, mass shooters, slave owners, pimps, drug dealers . . . just to name a few. Then there are the people who have personally wronged us. People who have been downright evil in their actions toward us. Do all these people deserve God's mercy? I guess a better question is, do we? I may not have done some of the evil I have witnessed or experienced, but I have still hurt others and offended God through my sin. I am still guilty and in need of forgiveness. This is one of the key lessons God teaches us through Jonah: none of us deserve grace, and yet he extends it to us anyway.

This week, I'm going to ask you to do something that could be really hard. I am going to ask you to pray for one of your "Ninevites"—one of your enemies—as a way to practice extending grace and mercy toward someone who doesn't deserve it. Before you get mad at me for this week's practice, you should know that I'm not the only one who thinks you should do this. Jesus also tells us to love our enemies and pray for those who persecute us (Matthew 5:44). It's hard to do, though. Really hard. In fact, I knew I was going to ask you to do this, and last night I had a dream about one of my enemies. I guess I know who I'm supposed to be praying for.

To help you discern the person to pray for, start by asking the Lord to bring someone to mind. Take some time to allow the Holy Spirit to work. You may be surprised who pops into your mind. It could be someone who has outright wronged you ages ago or someone you are in current conflict with. A word of caution: this is going to be harder on some of us than others. Some of us have lived through terrible atrocities and injustices at the hands of another. Please know that praying for them does not necessarily mean allowing that person back into your life. Further, if praying for that person could cause you psychological harm, please, with the Lord's guidance, choose someone else. One more word of caution: if you are in an ongoing abusive situation, please seek the help of a trusted friend, pastor, or counselor. Extending grace and mercy does not mean subjecting ourselves to the abuse of another.

Once you've settled on your person, commit to praying for them with intentionality every day this week. Pray however the Lord leads, but do so with the intention of seeking God's grace and mercy for them, just as he extended it to the Ninevites. If they don't know Jesus, you might also consider praying that they come to know him and live surrendered to him. However you pray, know that the Lord is holding you and loving you while you do it. You may also want to end your time of prayer with praises, acknowledging what the Lord has done for you and the ways he has extended grace and mercy to you.

You can do it, friend. I'm doing it right alongside you.

"To be a Christian means to forgive the inexcusable because God has forgiven the inexcusable in you."

—C. S. Lewis[1]

Day 2
Results of Obedience

Read Jonah 4:1–3.

Jonah went to Nineveh and preached his message which led to mass repentance. This might be one of the most effective sermons ever preached, yet Jonah did not appreciate the success.

1. Jonah relented and obeyed God. Why was he hesitant in the first place? What was the outcome of his obedience? How did Jonah feel about this?

History tells us the repentance of the Ninevites was short lived at best. Jonah's prophecy of destruction due to their violence and arrogance came to fruition and Nineveh was overthrown in 612 BC, which is about 150 years after Jonah was there. The book of Nahum chronicles Nineveh's demise. So why did God send Jonah to do this maddening task if they would eventually turn back to their evil ways? Surely God knew Nineveh would repent, but that it wouldn't last. To me, this points to the bigger picture of the story, which is about brave obedience no matter the outcome.

2. Fill in the chart below detailing who obeyed, how they obeyed, and what happened as a result.

Verses	Who Obeyed	How They Obeyed	What Happened
Esther 4:14–16; 9:20–22			
Luke 22:39–42; 23:44–46			
Acts 1:8; 2:14, 40–41			
Acts 7:54–60	Stephen	Boldly told the truth about Jesus before the high priest and the Sanhedrin	

3. Reflecting on the chart above, what does this tell you about obedience and the outcome of obedience? How does this make you feel?

4. Pray and ask the Lord if there is something he is calling you to do as an act of obedience. What are the possible outcomes of this act of obedience? Are there any outcomes that you are afraid of or would make you angry?

Another reason theologians speculate that Jonah was so angry about the Ninevites' repentance was because of his deep hatred for this group of people—their ethnic background, not just their behaviors. Yes, they were evil and had been enemies of the Jews for ages. But could it also be because they were a different race, culture, and religion? Jonah was called to be a prophet long before he was called to be a foreign missionary. And as a prophet, he lived under the evil Jewish king Jeroboam II, to whom he was willing to preach God's truth. It wasn't until Jonah was called to widen his view of God's love and mercy and go to a people different from him that he struggled, resisted, and ran. When he finally relented, he still held out hope that these people were beyond saving. It's when God extended mercy to them, these foreign people, that Jonah's anger flared.

Jonah has much to teach us about our heart toward others. Are there people we believe are beyond God's mercy? Are there people we believe *should be* beyond God's mercy? And if so, why do we believe this about some people and not others? If we can answer that honestly, what does that say about some of the Jonah-like tendencies we may be harboring?

5. Take a moment to reflect on where you, like Jonah, may hold biases toward others. Write out a prayer asking the Lord to help you see people as he does and to forgive you for any biases you hold.

If you haven't done so already, spend a few
minutes intentionally praying for your enemy.
Consider praying specifically that they
would come to know Jesus for the first time,
or come to know him in a deeper way
if they already know him.

Day 3
Who We Say He Is

Review Jonah 4:1–3.

6. Look up the following verses and write what Jonah declared about God in each verse. What do you think this says about Jonah's understanding of who God is?

Jonah 1:9

Jonah 2:9

Jonah 4:2

7. Jonah quoted Exodus 34:6–7. Read and compare it with Jonah 4:2. What differences do you notice? What did Jonah leave out? Why do you think he left this out?

Jonah spoke truth about God; he just didn't speak the whole truth. While the text doesn't make it clear if he left out parts of Exodus on purpose, it's certainly interesting that he did. In fact, it's a temptation many of us can fall into if we take just one truth about God without also remembering the whole truth of who he is. Done carelessly, this can go to the extreme of making God into whoever we want him to be in that moment: judge, healer, forgiver, provider, protector, and so on. Truthfully, he is all of these things, but he is all of them at the same time. He is never just a judge without also being a grace-filled forgiver. This is one of the reasons why it's critical for us to know and understand the whole story of Scripture—so we know and embrace and understand the truth of who our God is. Without knowing the whole truth, half-truths can creep in and lead us astray.

8. Read Matthew 4:1–11. Who used half-truths about God in these verses? What did he specifically do in verse 6? How did Jesus respond to each of the enemy's temptations?

9. Here are a couple of things I've heard people attribute to Scripture that aren't actually in the Bible.

God helps those who help themselves. Truth: While there is certainly work for us to do, we can't help ourselves at all when it comes to salvation (Ephesians 2:8–9).

God will never give you more than you can handle. Truth: If we could handle everything, we wouldn't need God (Philippians 4:13; Hebrews 4:15–16).

Money is the root of evil. Truth: It's actually the love of money that leads us astray. Money is neither good nor bad (1 Timothy 6:10).

What would you add to the list? Where have you witnessed people using half-truths about God? How has studying God's Word helped you combat these half-truths? How does this encourage you to make studying God's Word a priority in your life?

10. Do you think Jonah was intentional when he left out part of the truth about God? Why or why not? How might that have affected the Ninevites' view of God?

If you haven't done so already, spend a few
minutes intentionally praying for your enemy.
Consider praying specifically that they
would experience God's mercy and be
blessed in whatever they are doing today.

Day 4
Questioning God

Read Jonah 4:4–11.

Jonah left Nineveh, went outside the city, and built a shelter to
sit under to wait to see what God would do. Apparently Jonah's
shelter-building skills were inadequate because the Lord stepped
in to provide more shade.

11. Read Jonah 4:5–8 below and circle the three times the
    phrase "God provided" is used.

    Jonah had gone out and sat down at a place east of
    the city. There he made himself a shelter, sat in its
    shade and waited to see what would happen to the
    city. Then the LORD God provided a leafy plant and
    made it grow up over Jonah to give shade for his head
    to ease his discomfort, and Jonah was very happy
    about the plant. But at dawn the next day God pro-
    vided a worm, which chewed the plant so that it with-
    ered. When the sun rose, God provided a scorching
    east wind, and the sun blazed on Jonah's head so that
    he grew faint. He wanted to die, and said, "It would
    be better for me to die than to live."

Now fill in the chart below about these three things God provided in this passage.

What God Provided	What Happened	How Jonah Responded

Jonah's shelter was intended to provide relief from the heat of the day, but apparently it wasn't adequate because when the Lord provided a leafy plant to shade Jonah, he was overjoyed. Then, when the plant died, Jonah became so angry, he said he wanted to die. Jonah's emotions were wildly out of proportion with reality. He was sitting on the sidelines waiting for the city to be incinerated—for a hundred and twenty thousand people to lose their lives—and all he could think about was finding a comfortable spot to witness it from. Jonah's immature, self-centered nature is exposed, and it is here that God instructs him.

12. Write out on the following page the two questions God asked Jonah. What does each question pertain to? Why do you think God asked Jonah these questions?

Question 1 (verse 9):

Question 2 (verse 11):

13. Whom did Jonah direct his anger toward? Do you feel he was justified in his anger? Why or why not?

While the text doesn't tell us explicitly, I think it's safe to say that Jonah felt intense anger because his expectations were not met. He never wanted to go to the Ninevites. And when he finally did, he must have reasoned that there was no way these people would abandon their evil ways. Yet they did. And this not only dashed his expectations but made him livid.

14. How did God respond to Jonah and his anger?

"Here we see God's righteousness and love working together. He is both too holy and too loving to either destroy Jonah or to allow Jonah to remain as he is, and God is also too holy and too loving to allow us to remain as we are."

—Timothy Keller[2]

When I've felt angry with God, it's been because of my own unmet expectations. We may not even realize we have certain expectations for our lives and the lives of others until we get our toes stepped on. It's then, when something isn't going according to our plans, that our own anger toward God can flare up.

When my youngest daughter went through depression, we were at a loss for what to do. We tried everything. And then finally, with medical help and counseling, she started to get better. On the advice of her doctor, we sent her to summer camp with the belief that being outdoors and playing would be good for her soul. And it was. Until she shared her story and the camp became fearful that she would hurt herself, which she wouldn't have, and sent her home. I remember getting the call from the camp and feeling anger toward them and then toward God. I fell to my face and wept as I cried out, Why, God? Why would you take something so good and potentially healing from her? I wrestled with God through tears, anger, and fear as we made the six-hour drive to go get her.

I tell you this story because we will all have moments that land us on our face before God wondering, Why, God? We may never get answers to these questions, but I assure you, God can handle them. We still don't know why he allowed this to happen to our daughter, but we do know that, against all odds, he used it for good in her life. If you hear her tell the story, which she gladly does, she will tell you that this was a pivotal moment for her. You see, when she climbed into the back seat and started to cry, she realized she could feel again and those tears gave her hope that she was getting better. I would have never chosen this for her—I still wouldn't. But ultimately, we have to trust that God knows best. Even if and even when our stories don't end with what feels like a happy ending.

The important thing to remember in wrestling through our anger with God is that we can't get stuck there. It's important to process through the anger, no matter how long it takes, and move to a place where we can remember and proclaim what is true about our God—that he is a good and loving Father (Psalm 103) and that he will use all things for our good (Romans 8:28; Jeremiah 29:11).

15. Have you ever felt anger toward God because of something that happened or didn't happen in your life? Describe the event that caused your anger. Were you able to move through this anger? If so, how?

If you are still feeling anger toward God, consider intentionally trying one of your group members' methods that they share in small group to help you move through your anger. Also consider reaching out to a trusted friend, pastor, or counselor to pray with and talk openly about how you are feeling.

16. How did God use the plant as an object lesson for Jonah? What was Jonah most concerned about and why? What was God most concerned about and why?

17. How did God describe the 120,000 Ninevites (verse 11)? What do you think this means? Read Luke 23:34. In this passage Jesus is hanging on the cross and as he is dying, he looks down upon his tormentors and states these words. How does this passage help you understand God's heart toward people like the Ninevites?

It's important to note that while someone may be ignorant to the ways of God, that does not give them a free pass to do as they want. Evil is still evil. There will come a day when Jesus will return to set everything right. All that is broken will be made whole. Evil will be fully and finally banished at that time, and all who are found to be without faith in Jesus will be judged fully and finally for their actions (Revelation 20:11–15).

If you haven't done so already, spend a few
minutes intentionally praying for your enemy.
Consider praying specifically that relationships
in their life would be life-giving and full of peace
and love.

Day 5
Receiving and Extending Mercy

Review Jonah 4:10–11.

The story of Jonah ends abruptly. We don't get to hear Jonah's
response to God's question or find out what happened next.
However, we can make a few assumptions. First, a story with
this much detail, especially the parts that only Jonah would
know, had to be relayed by Jonah to others. Second, since Jonah
was willing to tell the full and honest story about his disobedience and running—including endangering the lives of innocent
sailors, being thrown into a stormy sea rather than obey God,
being upset about God's mercy, and his immature tantrum about
a plant—he must have learned at least a few lessons as a result. If
he learned nothing, we would assume he wouldn't have told the
story because it certainly doesn't cast him in a favorable light.

One of the lessons Jonah learned was about how God loves all
people and wants to show them grace and mercy.

18. God told Jonah the Ninevites didn't know their right hand
from their left. In what ways was this also an accurate description of Jonah?

According to Romans 3:22–24, how is this also an accurate description of us and everyone around us? How do we receive God's mercy today?

19. Read 2 Peter 3:8–9. What is the Lord's ultimate desire for all people? As a result of his desire, describe God's level of patience with us. How does the truth in these verses encourage or challenge you today? Write a prayer of thanksgiving or confession to God about this.

There are two kinds of repentance. The first is seen in 2 Peter 3:8–9, which is a one-time repentance of turning to Jesus in faith and placing our trust in him alone as the only way we can be saved. The second kind of repentance is ongoing. It is when we agree with God about our sin and turn back to him and his will for us (Luke 11:4; 1 John 1:9). This second kind of repentance is continually needed because we will struggle with sin until the day we die.

20. In the table on the next page, look back over the story of Jonah and list some of the places where you think Jonah needed to repent for his actions. Next to each action, list what you think might have been the underlying heart posture that could have led Jonah to that action.

Action to Repent From	Heart Posture
Jonah ran from the Lord toward Tarshish (1:3)	Possibly anger and hatred toward an ethnic and religious group different from his own

21. Prayerfully reflect on the list above and ask the Lord to help you see what is in your heart that could be holding you back from boldly following where God is leading you (some examples could be pride, anger, busyness, bias, or idols such as money, comfort, or status). Knowing God gives us the same mercy and forgiveness he gave Jonah, confess this to God and write a prayer asking him to help you change your heart posture to be one of trust only in him.

22. Ultimately, what do you think Jonah learned about God and himself as a result of this experience? How do you think this changed how he lived the rest of his life?

23. Through studying Jonah, what one or two key lessons have you learned or been reminded of about God? How does this (or should this) change how you live your life moving forward?

PRACTICE REFLECTION

1. Did you intentionally pray for your "Ninevite" this week? If so, what did you notice about your heart toward them as you prayed? If not, why?

2. What was this prayer practice like for you? Did it reveal anything to you about yourself, God, or your enemy?

3. How does knowing that God extended the same grace and mercy toward the Ninevites as he did toward Jonah help you as you seek to love your enemy and pray for those who persecute you (Matthew 5:44)?

YOU ARE CALLED

Day 1
Practice—Seeking God's Will

Earlier in this study we saw that Esther was clearly called by God, providentially placed in a time and place in history to do something that only she could do. Circumstance after circumstance opened door after door for her to have her "for such a time as this" moment. It's even more clear that Jonah was called by God. Jonah heard the unmistakable voice of God inviting him to a task he did not want to do. He resisted and ran. When he finally relented, he was angry with God for his grace toward the undeserving.

Two very different circumstances. Two very different people. Two very different callings. Yet the very same God.

We, too, have been called by God. Just like Esther and Jonah, we have been providentially placed in a time and place in history to do things that only we can do. Many of us long to have the clarity of calling that Jonah received, although I'm pretty sure we would all pass on the task of going to Nineveh. By God's grace, sometimes we do get this kind of clarity.

I'll never forget the moment when God invited me to take a bold step of obedience by going to seminary. It did feel like an almost audible voice, but that's the only time it's ever happened like that for me. Most of our invitations to follow God are more in line with what Esther received. When she stood at her crossroads moment, it was her circumstances, trusted advisors, and unique position that pointed her toward the path that only she could take. We can use similar indicators, along with prayer guided by the Holy Spirit, to help us discern our next steps when we are at our own crossroads. God may seem mysterious to us at times, but he will never make his will a mystery. If we seek to know his will and desire to follow it, he will be faithful to show us how he is calling us to follow him.

This week, I want to invite you into a process of earnestly seeking to know God's will for you. To do this, we are going to practice something we saw in both Jonah and Esther: fasting and prayer. I realize we did a fasting exercise a few weeks ago, but this time I want to invite you to fast with the express intention of seeking his will for your life. I'd also like to invite you to fast from food. There are legitimate reasons why some of us cannot fast from food, so if it would be unhealthy for you to do this fast, please prayerfully decide what else you can fast from that could have a similar impact.

To do this fast, choose a day or two this week when you can fast from a meal or for a whole day. If you are doing a meal, I recommend you eat a normal breakfast and then break your fast with a normal dinner. If you are fasting for a whole day, I recommend you do a sundown to sundown fast where you fast from after dinner one evening to breaking the fast with dinner the next evening. Don't forget to drink lots of water throughout the day. Fasting from food will do a few things for us. First, it creates physical pangs and longings in our body that are hard to ignore. Use these physical cues as reminders to seek the Lord earnestly and boldly every time you feel them. Second, by not taking time to prepare and eat a meal, we open up additional time in our day. Use the time you would have spent preparing or getting food and eating it as a time of intentional prayer.

Fasting is often a communal act. Esther asked the people to fast with her. The city of Nineveh fasted corporately to beg God for mercy. The early church fasted together before they made decisions (Acts 14:23). With that in mind, we will use our fast to seek God's will for both our own lives as well as the women in our group. I encourage you to write down all their names, and one by one ask God to reveal his will to each of them and to give them bold courage to follow. Pray the same prayer for yourself and then spend some time silently listening for what the Lord may want to say to you. If you feel a nudge from the Spirit about something he wants you to do, write it down so you can remember it and continue praying about it. But do more than pray. If you believe God is placing you at a crossroads moment and inviting you to follow him in some new way, take a cue from Esther and share it with some of your "trusted advisors" so they can help you discern God's will in this matter. And then if you feel like God is calling you forward, be brave and bold and take the leap of faithful obedience. For who knows, maybe this is one of your "for such a time as this" moments.

You have been called by God. He has chosen you and gifted you to fulfill a calling. He has created good work for you. Will you follow him?

If you haven't already, choose a day or two to fast and intentionally pray to seek the Lord's direction for your and your group's next steps of obedience.

Day 2
Created on Purpose for a Purpose

Read Psalm 139:13–16.

At this point in our study, I hope we can all emphatically state that Esther and Jonah were called by God to do something only they could do. I think we often see with greater clarity what others have been called by God to do than we see it for ourselves. For example, when I see my senior pastor step up to lead with grace and wisdom in uncertain times, I have a deep sense that he has been clearly called by God to his role. Or when an author brings words to life in a way that changes my heart, I silently thank God that he created them to do that work. Or when my girls were little and one of their teachers noticed them and loved them well, I was certain that teaching was exactly what they had been gifted to do. But when it comes to my calling, I'm a lot more uncertain. And as I've talked with women over the years, I've learned I am not alone in this uncertainty.

So where do we start in the process of discerning what the Lord may be calling us to? I think the first place we need to start is with a reminder to our heart that we've been created on purpose and for a purpose. Every single one of us. Me and you.

Nothing about how God put you together is a mistake. He decided the color of your hair and the texture of your toenails. You aren't just a random mix of cells that happened to come together. God is not surprised by anything about you. This is one reason we need to resist negative self-talk. When we tear ourselves down, we tear our creator down. Thus, the first step to embracing our calling is to understand the care and intention that we've been created with.

1. According to Psalm 139:13–15, who created us and how? How are we supposed to respond to God about who he's made us to be?

2. Write down at least five things you appreciate about how God made you (physical or personality traits). Then take a few minutes to write a prayer of thanksgiving to God, praising him for these things.

3. Psalm 139:16 tells us that God ordains the number of our days. What does that mean to you? How does thinking about God knowing the number of your days impact how you think about following him no matter where he calls you?

4. Read and write out Ephesians 2:10. While it may feel like busywork to look up a verse and then transcribe it in your own hand, I believe it isn't. This is a tool the Lord uses in my life to help me slow down so I can really notice his words. Every. Single. One. Can I encourage you to give it a try? As you do, slow down and notice each word and perhaps take note of what stands out to you. If you're ever struggling to stay focused on God's Word (we all have those days), come back to this as a tool to help you settle your mind and refocus your heart on truth. Circle or underline the words that stand out to you. Why do you think these particular words stand out to you?

Studies also show that writing things out by hand is a powerful tool for our memory. It helps us retain information, comprehend new ideas, and increase our productivity. I'd say that's a good return on investment for putting pencil to paper instead of just tapping out everything on our keyboards. Try it this week and see if you find if any of these results are true for you.[1]

· · · · · ·

5. The original Greek word translated as *handiwork* in Ephesians 2:10 is *poiema*, which is where we get the word *poem*. If you've never talked with a poet about how they craft their work, let me tell you that it's a long, strenuous, thought-filled process. Being God's *poiema* means we are beautiful, multidimensional words with flesh that God crafted and smoothed before releasing into the world. What does this

convey to you about being God's handiwork? What have we been created to do? When were these works prepared for us? How does this make you feel?

Ephesians 2:10 has always provided great comfort and encouragement to me. It tells me I don't have to play a game of spiritual "Where's Waldo?" to try to uncover some sort of good work to do. Rather, God has already created and prepared all the good works for me. Because he's prepared them and he knows me better than anyone, they're perfectly suited to me. While that doesn't mean the work will always be easy or even successful by my terms, I can rest in knowing that God is leading and directing my steps the whole way. My role is to prayerfully seek him and then obediently follow. The rest is up to him.

PRACTICE REMINDER

If you haven't already, choose a day or two to fast and intentionally pray to seek the Lord's direction for your and your group's next steps of obedience.

Day 3
Collectively Called

Read Matthew 22:36–39, 28:18–20.

Now that we've taken some time to think about how we've been created—on purpose and for a purpose—let's shift to explore how we are called by God to serve him in specific ways. First, I want to dispel a myth many people have about callings: your calling isn't a needle in a haystack hunt for the one thing you are supposed to discover and do for the rest of your life. I mean, I guess that could happen, but it's not my or most people's experience. Callings change and grow; they ebb and flow. Some callings are bigger and longer, like my calling to be in vocational ministry as a pastor. Some callings are smaller and more embedded into our lives, like my calling to love my neighbor well by reaching out to her today. Some callings are temporary, like going on a mission trip. Some callings are lifelong, like being a disciple of Jesus. We are chosen by God to do many things over the course of our lives. In order to constantly follow where he leads, we need to maintain a vital and loving relationship with him.

It's also important to note that there are some things that God collectively calls us all to and some things that he specifically calls only you to. First, let's explore our collective calling by seeing what Jesus said the most important things are for us to do.

6. In Matthew 22:36–39 an expert in religious law asked Jesus, "Which is the greatest commandment in the Law?" How did Jesus respond in verse 37? How do you think these three aspects of ourselves differ? How are they the same?

In other passages that are similar to this one, loving the Lord with all our strength is also included (Deuteronomy 6:5; Mark 12:30). While there are differences in how we love God with these specific aspects of ourselves, many think that Jesus was really just trying to drive home the point that we need to love God with our entire being.

7. According to John 14:23, how do we show our love for God? What are some ways you can know God's teaching? How do you, or can you, make knowing God's Word a priority in your life?

8. In Matthew 22:39, what does Jesus add to the first and greatest commandment? Why do you think he answered the question in this order? Do you struggle to love yourself? How could this translate into how you should love others?

The first part of our collective calling is to follow the Great Commandment and love God above anything and everyone, and then to love others as we love ourselves. It's simple to say, but hard to do. For me, there are all kinds of things that compete for my love and attention. Things that want to consume my heart, mind, and soul. Keeping God front and center as my first love and primary devotion happens only when I keep my heart and mind intentionally focused on him. And just to be clear, that's really hard to do. It is only by the grace of God that any of us can keep him front and center in our lives. I pray daily, sometimes multiple times a day, that the Lord would help me stay focused on him. The good news is, God longs to help us with this. All we need to do is ask (Psalm 145:18). And when we wander off course, which we will, we need to give ourselves some grace then turn our eyes back to Jesus.

Let's explore the second part of our collective calling, the Great Commission (Matthew 28:18–20), which contains some of Jesus's last recorded words. These words serve as a final send-off and directive for Jesus's followers, which includes us.

9. Read Matthew 28:18–20. Write down all the things Jesus told the disciples—including us—to do. What promise did he make to them and us at the end of the verses? What are some ways you have or are following this call?

10. Jesus says we are to baptize new disciples. Have you ever been baptized? What was this experience like for you? If you haven't been baptized, why not?

If you haven't been baptized, can I encourage you to get baptized as soon as you can? Jesus clearly tells us this is something all of his followers should do and thus it falls into this collective calling category. Just like we don't need to wonder if we should love our neighbor, we also don't need to wonder if we should be baptized. As we are in the process of seeking to discern God's next steps, this would be a perfect next step to take. Make an appointment with your pastor to discuss this with them.

11. Prayerfully consider your collective calling found in the Great Commandment and the Great Commission. What are some practical ways you feel like God is inviting you to live out this part of your calling this week?

If you haven't already, choose a day or two to fast and intentionally pray to seek the Lord's direction for your and your group's next steps of obedience.

Day 4
Specifically Called

Read Romans 12:6–8, 1 Corinthians 12:7–11.

Now let's turn to our individual and specific callings. Just like Esther and Jonah, we have been placed in a certain time and place in history, given unique gifts and skills, and invited into specific opportunities to serve God and his people. To help us discover what some of these opportunities may be, let's start by exploring what Scripture says are some of the specific gifts God gives to believers.

"God designed each of us so that there would be no duplication in the world. No one has the exact same mix of factors that make you unique. That means no one else on earth will ever be able to play the role God has planned for you."

—Rick Warren[2]

12. Read the verses below and circle each of the gifts named.

We have different gifts, according to the grace given to each of us. If your gift is prophesying, then prophesy in accordance with your faith; if it is serving, then serve; if it is teaching, then teach; if it is to encourage,

then give encouragement; if it is giving, then give gen-
erously; if it is to lead, do it diligently; if it is to show
mercy, do it cheerfully. (Romans 12:6–8)

Now to each one the manifestation of the Spirit is
given for the common good. To one there is given
through the Spirit a message of wisdom, to another
a message of knowledge by means of the same Spirit,
to another faith by the same Spirit, to another gifts
of healing by that one Spirit, to another miraculous
powers, to another prophecy, to another distinguish-
ing between spirits, to another speaking in different
kinds of tongues, and to still another the interpretation of tongues. All these are the work of one and the
same Spirit, and he distributes them to each one, just
as he determines. (1 Corinthians 12:7–11)

According to 1 Corinthians 12:7, why are the gifts given?
What does this tell you about how you are to use your spiritual gifts?

Each of the New Testament passages that list spiritual gifts are
slightly different from each other (Romans 12:6–8; 1 Corinthians
12:7–11, 28–30; Ephesians 4:11–13). This leads us to believe that
the lists are not meant to be exhaustive. Because of this, taking
a multiple-choice quiz to discover your spiritual gifts won't necessarily uncover the specific gifts that God could give you. There
are online assessments like this, and while they can be helpful and
affirming, I recommend you don't get hung up on taking multiple
tests to decide what your gift is. Instead, jump in to volunteering
in your church or community and just try some things that seem
like they might be a good fit for you. It's also helpful to reflect on

what you are good at and enjoy doing. When the things you are doing are for the common good in building up the body of Christ (Ephesians 4:12), or help us express love to our neighbors, that's a great clue that these things could be your spiritual gifts.

13. What are some things you currently enjoy doing or enjoyed doing in the past? (If you are struggling to come up with ideas, go back to your childhood and think about what you used to dream about doing when you grew up, or think about school and what you were good at, or other places you have found joy in doing things.) How are or were these things received by others? (Were they appreciated, did it help someone, did anyone notice?)

14. According to the verses we read in question 12, as well as what you are good at and enjoy doing, what do you think your spiritual gifts could be? Why do you think this?

15. How could you potentially use these gifts and other abilities you may have for the common good or to build up the body of Christ? Take a moment to brainstorm how you could do this and write your ideas below.

Another potential arrow that God can use to point us toward what he's calling us to is paying attention to issues and broken places in our world that stir our hearts. He did this with Esther, who was heartbroken over the fact that her people would perish if she chose to do nothing. God had placed her in a position where she was uniquely situated to do something . . . and this led her to take the risk to do what only she could do.

16. What are some of the issues and broken places in our world that break your heart? (Some topics to get the ideas flowing: abuse, marginalization, injustice, bias, chaos, scarcity, brokenness.) Why do you think you are drawn to these issues?

17. As you consider your gifts from question 14 along with the places in our world that break your heart from question 16, are there any ways that these two could overlap? Prayerfully ask the Lord to help you see how he might be inviting you to combine these two things for his glory. Write down any ideas that come to mind.

I think it's also worth stating the obvious here: we don't always get to make an impact in the places that stir our hearts. Jonah is a great example of this. God called him to do work that he was specifically gifted and equipped to do, but which he didn't want to do. Sometimes obedience is like that. Sometimes we have to do what we are called to do simply because God is telling us to.

There's a myth I want to dispel before we leave this section and that revolves around the sacred versus secular work divide. Some of us are called to serve God overtly in vocational ministry, and others are called to serve him in secular spaces. But this secular versus sacred divide is something we created, not God. All work that God leads us to and that is done for his glory is sacred work. For example, my husband is an applied mathematician who creates and builds programs to help the airlines land their planes on time. If you've ever landed on time, you know how much glory you give Jesus for that. Truly, though, God gave my husband a mind that thinks and solves problems in this way, and as he does his job with excellence, he gives God glory. I believe God delights in my husband's good work, just as God delights in yours.

However, we also need to recognize that there are times when we do work that doesn't feel like it matches with the gifts and skills God has given us. While these tasks and roles may not align with our calling, we can still glorify God by doing them with excellence and joy. And then perhaps we serve him more overtly with our gifts in other places.

The important thing to remember is that when God calls us to serve him, it is sacred work regardless of the setting we serve him in. So, whether that's stocking shelves, educating children, teaching the Bible, or launching a rocket to Mars, when we use the gifts, skills, and talents we have for his glory, he delights in that.

As we seek to discover our next steps, know that they may be embedded in what you are already doing. But it's also possible God is calling you to make some changes. Either way, he will guide and lead you. Keep pressing on, exploring his Word, and praying boldly for him to show you your next step. He will be faithful to answer your prayers.

If you haven't already, choose a day or two to fast and intentionally pray to seek the Lord's direction for your and your group's next steps of obedience.

Day 5
Your Next Step

Read Proverbs 3:5–6.

As you continue to discern your next steps, don't forget to look around you and notice what opportunities are present. This is often how God points us toward what he wants us to do. When our giftings match opportunities, it's a natural win. When this happens, take some time to pray about if this could be your next step. There's a good chance it is.

It's also helpful to invite trusted advisors to pray and process with you—discernment is not a solo sport. I think a lot of Christians can get into trouble if they feel a sense of leading from the Lord but then never consult other trusted believers. God gives us Christian brothers and sisters to help us in the discernment process; they are like guardrails that help us stay on track to make sure we are hearing him correctly.

Hearing God clearly can sometimes be difficult because our own needs, wants, and desires can at times drown out or over-shadow God's voice. Often these needs, wants, and desires are not against God's will, but sometimes they aren't exactly what he's inviting us into. Let me give you a quick example. In my years of pastoral ministry, I've had many conversations with women who feel called to teach other women. I think this can be a godly and noble desire. But often as I dig further, it becomes apparent that some aren't willing to do the hard work to learn how to teach and how to rightly handle God's Word. They also aren't willing to be patient and take opportunities to teach smaller groups of women as a starting place. This helps me see that these desires are perhaps misplaced and then I can lovingly redirect and encourage them to spend some more time with the Lord to discern what he is calling them to.

On the other hand, I've had this same conversation with women who are now doing the hard work of preparation for this noble task. What a gift to walk alongside both of these types of women and be one of many who speak into their lives. The bottom line is, they want to follow God's leading and for that I am grateful.

This isn't to dissuade you from boldly following God. Rather, it is to invite you to be wise as you seek the counsel of others who will take seriously the call to pray with you and help you discern God's next steps.

18. Reflecting back over this lesson and our whole study, if anything were possible, what is one thing you would love to do to serve God? How would this change the life you are currently living?

19. What are some of the things that scare you about surrendering to and following God? Are any of these fears realistic? If they are, how would you deal with them? Even if something you fear did happen, why would following God still be worth the sacrifice?

PRACTICE REFLECTION

1. Were you able to participate in fasting and praying this week? If so, what was the experience like for you?

2. Did you sense the Lord's leading in any way? If so, what do you think he is leading you to?

3. Based on this lesson and your prayer and fasting this week, what next steps of obedience do you believe the Lord is inviting you to take? Fill in the blank below to write out your next step.

   I believe the Lord is calling me to take this next bold step of obedience:

   _____

   What excites you about this? What makes you nervous?

4. Prayerfully make a plan for who you will ask to help you discern these next steps and what other actions you will take. Write it below.

My prayerful plan of action is:

_____

_____

If you are able, pray this prayer of commitment and thanksgiving to God:

Lord, thank you that as I stand at this crossroads, I know that you have chosen me and called me to do good work for your glory. By your grace and through your strength, I say yes to what I believe you have laid on my heart as my next bold step of obedience. As I share with those around me, give them wisdom to help me discern if this is your will. I trust you to carry me and empower me as I follow you. I leave the results of my obedience in your hands, and I will give you the glory for anything good that comes as a result. I also trust that true joy and lasting peace are only found in walking closely with you. Even if the journey is hard, I will turn to you to supply me with all I need along the way. Thank you for choosing me as your beloved daughter. Thank you for calling me to do this good work. Amen.

Well done, friend. You finished well, and I'm so proud of you.

I can't wait to hear your stories. Like Esther and Jonah, we will continually be placed at our own crossroads and invited to follow God. May you always choose faithful obedience to him. It makes a lasting impact on our world. So let's get out there and bravely follow wherever he leads us.

After all, who knows but that you have come to this place for such a time as this?

ACKNOWLEDGMENTS

I'll start with Esther. Thank you for being a real woman who stared down her fear and saved a nation. You did not get to choose the life you lived, but you lived it well and you are an example and encouragement to me.

Jonah, thank you for making sure your story was told—even though it was, at times, less than flattering. I'm grateful, because fleeing to Tarshish happens more than I'd like to admit. Your story reveals God's relentless and loving pursuit of his people, and I take great comfort in that.

Thank you to Irving Bible Church. First, to the women for studying God's Word with me. You are an incredible community. Second, to Barry and Bryan for believing that writing is worth my effort and time. I'm grateful for brothers like you who pray for and invest in me.

Thank you to the incredible editing team at Kregel—Janyre, Sarah, and Joel. What a privilege it is to work with you amazing people. Your fingerprints are all over this study, and I know it brings God glory. So thankful for the gifts he has given each of you.

Thank you to the many friends who read all these words and helped me refine them—Candice, Sissy, Tiffany, Kat, Amy, Betsy, and Lisa. You are treasures. Who gives so much so freely? You do!

Thank you to Tim, my love. And to Taylor and Billie, my heart. You're all a lot like Esther. When you stand at your crossroads, don't forget that.

And mostly, thank you to Jesus. I'm still stunned by who you are and what you've done for me.

NOTES

Week 1: Esther Becomes Queen

1. Karen H. Jobes, *The NIV Application Commentary: Esther* (Grand Rapids: Zondervan, 1999), 43.
2. Sharifa Stevens, "Vashti: Dishonored for Having Honor," in Sandra Glahn, ed., *Vindicating the Vixens: Revisiting Sexualized, Vilified, and Marginalized Women of the Bible* (Grand Rapids: Kregel, 2017), 239.
3. Jobes, *Esther*, 96.
4. Joyce G. Baldwin, *Esther: An Introduction and Commentary*, vol. 12 (Downers Grove, IL: InterVarsity, 1984), 66.
5. Baldwin, *Esther*, 67–68.
6. Warren W. Wiersbe, *Be Committed* (Wheaton, IL: Victor, 1993), 90.

Week 2: Edict of Death

1. Volume of Proceedings of the Fourth International Congregational Council, held in Boston, Massachusetts, June 29–July 6, 1920, address delivered July 5, 1920, to the International Congregational Council, "Some Present Features of the Temperance Crusade" by Sir R. Murray Hyslop, JP [The National Council of the Congregational Churches of the United States, New York] (Boston: Pilgrim Press, 1921), 166.
2. Warren W. Wiersbe, *Be Committed* (Wheaton, IL: Victor, 1993), 92.

Week 3: Facing the Crossroads

1. Carolyn Custis James, *Lost Women of the Bible* (Grand Rapids: Zondervan, 2009), 152.
2. C. S. Lewis, *Mere Christianity* (New York: HarperCollins, 1952), 109.

3. Warren W. Wiersbe, *Be Committed* (Wheaton, IL: Victor, 1993), 124.
4. Karen H. Jobes, *The NIV Application Commentary: Esther* (Grand Rapids: Zondervan, 1999), 165.
5. Wiersbe, *Be Committed*, 141.

Week 5: Resisting and Running

1. James Bruckner, *The NIV Application Commentary: Jonah, Nahum, Habakkuk, Zephaniah* (Grand Rapids: Zondervan, 2004), 28–29.
2. Timothy Keller, *The Prodigal Prophet: Jonah and the Mystery of God's Mercy* (New York: Viking, 2018), 5.
3. Kevin Youngblood, *Exegetical Commentary on the Old Testament: Jonah* (Grand Rapids: Zondervan, 2013), 78.
4. Keller, *Prodigal Prophet*, 52.
5. Paul Mackrell, *Opening Up Jonah* (Leominster, UK: Day One, 2007), 44.

Week 6: Praise from the Depths

1. James Bruckner, *The NIV Application Commentary: Jonah, Nahum, Habakkuk, Zephaniah* (Grand Rapids: Zondervan, 2004), 83–84. Emphasis in original.
2. Paul Mackrell, *Opening Up Jonah* (Leominster, UK: Day One, 2007), 10.
3. Bruckner, *Jonah, Nahum, Habakkuk, Zephaniah*, 87.

Week 7: Jonah's Obedience and God's Compassion

1. James Bruckner, *The NIV Application Commentary: Jonah, Nahum, Habakkuk, Zephaniah* (Grand Rapids: Zondervan, 2004), 102.

Week 8: Our Ninevites

1. C. S. Lewis, *The Weight of Glory* (New York: HarperCollins, 2001), 183.
2. Timothy Keller, *The Prodigal Prophet: Jonah and the Mystery of God's Mercy* (New York: Viking, 2018), 132.

Week 9: You Are Called

1. Suzy Frisch, "Three Scientific Links Between Handwriting Your Notes and Memory," Redbooth, August 3, 2016, https://redbooth.com/blog/handwriting-and-memory.

2. Rick Warren, *The Purpose Driven Life* (Grand Rapids: Zondervan, 2002), 241.

ABOUT THE AUTHOR

Jodie Niznik is the women's and adult ministries pastor at Irving Bible Church in Irving, Texas. She has served in various roles on the pastoral team at her church over the last eleven years. Her calling and passion is to equip people to take the next step in their journey with Jesus. She loves to write about and teach scriptural truths in practical and easy-to-understand ways.

Jodie has an undergraduate degree in broadcast journalism from the University of Colorado and a master's degree in Christian education with an emphasis in women's ministry from Dallas Theological Seminary. She is also the author of *Choose: A Study of Moses for a Life That Matters* and *Trust: A Study of Joseph for Persevering Through Life's Challenges,* and the coauthor of *Galatians: Discovering Freedom in Christ Through Daily Practice* with Sue Edwards.

Jodie is married to Tim. They have two young adult daughters, Taylor and Billie. Jodie and Tim miss their daughters but love their quiet Saturdays. Jodie believes gummy bears and coffee are sweet gifts from the Lord that provide fuel as she writes Bible studies and prepares biblical teachings.